Product Development
and Architecture
Visions / Methods / Innovations

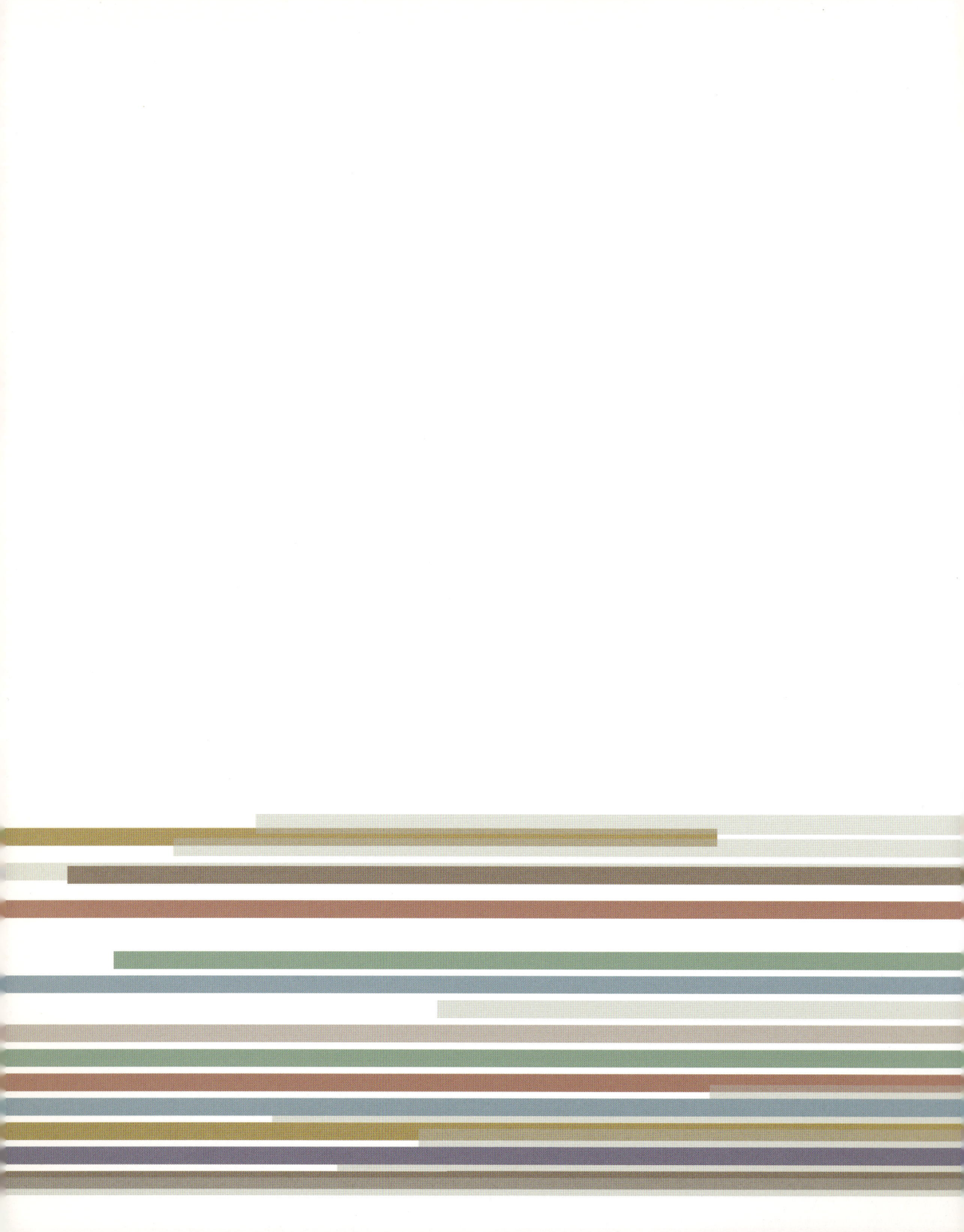

Uta Pottgiesser, Holger Strauß (eds.)

Product
Development and
Architecture
Visions / Methods / Innovations

Birkhäuser Basel

Contents

7   Preface

9   **Human-Centered Design:** A Focus on the Individual
Uta Pottgiesser

24   **Digital Architecture:** From Design to Production
Marco Hemmerling, Ulrich Nether

34   **Facade Road Map:** Paths and Pathfinders
Ulrich Knaack

Developing Ideas

53   **Curved Planes**
Christoph Schindler, Jan Bieniek
60   **The Rediscovery of Known Materials**
Christian Grabitz, Christina Kröger

Redefining Boundaries

69   **Total Building Envelope**
Winfried Heusler, Steve Lo
78   **Engineers Construct Art**
Thomas Henriksen

Expanding Networks

87   **Open Innovation**
Eckard Foltin, Lorenz Kramer, Holger Strauß
94   **Connections and Layers**
Christoph Kirch, Thomas Böhm

Conserving Resources

107   **Energy Supplying Envelope**
Jan Wurm
116   **Facade Recycling**
Linda Hildebrand, Daniel Arztmann
124   **Wohn-Vision-2020**
Verena Wriedt, Mark Fleischhauer

133   **Measuring Light – Calculating Geometry**
José Miguel Martínez Rico, Sergio Saiz Bombín, Aitor Leceta Murguzur

140   **Digital Design and Construction**
Marco Hemmerling, Jens Böke, Frank Püchner

148   **Optimizing and Directing Processes**
Xavier Ferrés Padró, Thomas Braig, Jörn Tillmanns

Optimizing Planning Tools

159   **The Printed Building Envelope**
Holger Strauß

168   **Direct Glass Fabrication**
Lisa Rammig

Transfering Technologies

176   Notes
179   Authors
182   Index
183   Acknowledgments
184   Imprint

Preface

A closer look at the processes involved in the progression from idea to invention to innovation assists in the discovery of suitable approaches and suitable responses to these issues. The introductory articles relate to the relevant fields of research and innovation for the built environment: design, computational methods, and product development.

The case studies selected are the result of interdisciplinary cooperation between universities, research institutions, engineers, architects, artists, and different companies. They demonstrate that the market success of ideas, visions, or products for the built environment is closely linked to an understanding of design issues and cultural experience. They represent examples of best practice for the design research and innovation system models presented here. They address the following questions:

> How did the different projects and teams find a creative and targeted method of communication and collaboration?
> What are the relevant topics of investigation and action for the built environment in the face of challenges such as climate change, resource and energy efficiency, and changing societies and markets?
> How are the projects triggered by different factors, technologies, and market needs?
> How can innovation in the built environment be fostered and increased?

Themes

Human-Centered Design:
A Focus on the Individual

Uta Pottgiesser

"Good architecture should be a projection of life itself and that implies an intimate knowledge of biological, social, technical, and artistic problems."
Walter Gropius

Challenges

Ever since the middle of the nineteenth century — when the negative consequences of industrialization became inescapably obvious — the improvement of human living conditions, in both social and environmental respects, has been considered to be a major concern of architecture and urban planning [1]. In spite of this, most buildings and built environments are designed without a detailed knowledge of all the effects of spaces, materials, and technologies on the perception and actions of their users. Now, in the early twenty-first century, almost a century after the Bauhaus was founded in Weimar in 1918, architecture — along with the new disciplines of interior architecture and design — is strongly influenced by the projected consequences of climate change and demographic change on our world and by the significantly different needs of a society with a rapidly growing and aging population. The disciplines of planning and design are faced with the question of what position to take and how best to contribute to resolving current problems in society. Quality of life and user comfort are key priorities, and an understanding of the impact of the built environment and of new technologies on human perception represents a strategic challenge in the design of spaces, buildings, and cities. The impact of the early twenty-first century technological and social innovations described by Nefiodow extends to the processes of design, planning, and manufacture and the training and labor market [2].

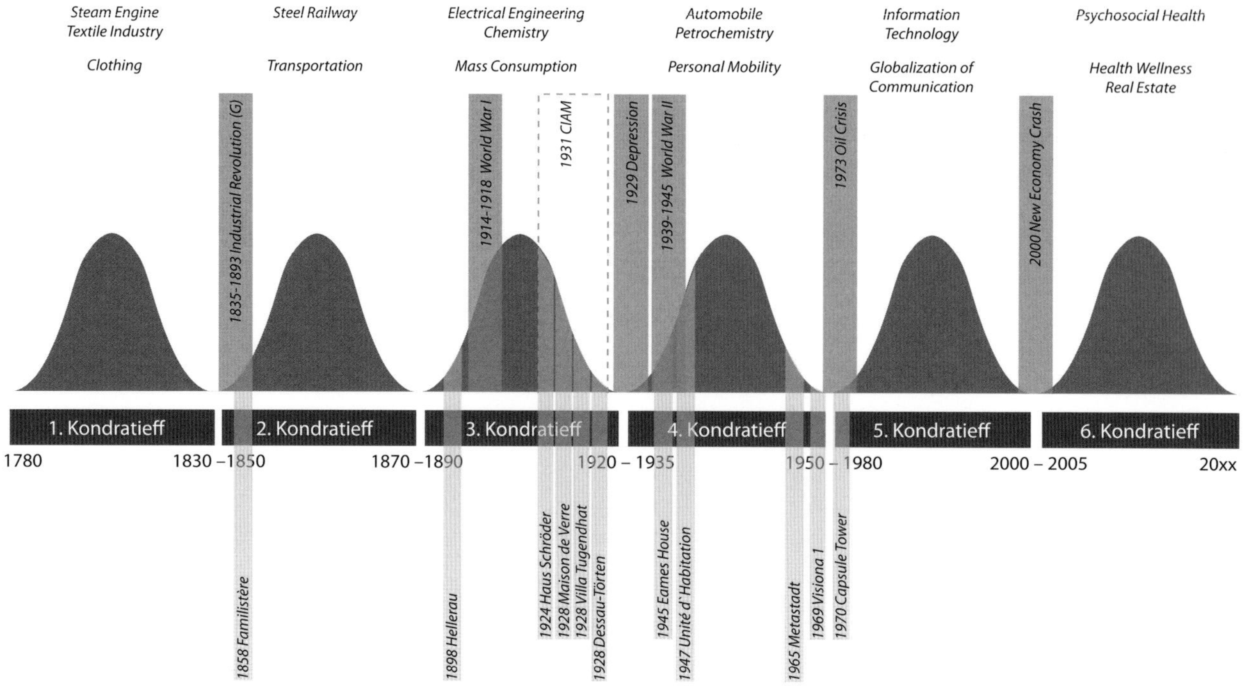

Steam Engine
Textile Industry
Clothing
Steel Railway
Transportation
Electrical Engineering
Chemistry
Mass Consumption
Automobile
Petrochemistry
Personal Mobility
Information
Technology
Globalization of
Communication
Psychosocial Health
Health Wellness
Real Estate
1835-1893 Industrial Revolution (G)
1914-1918 World War I
1931 CIAM
1929 Depression
1939-1945 World War II
1973 Oil Crisis
2000 New Economy Crash
1. Kondratieff
2. Kondratieff
3. Kondratieff
4. Kondratieff
5. Kondratieff
6. Kondratieff
1780
1830 – 1850
1870 – 1890
1920 – 1935
1950 – 1980
2000 – 2005
20xx
1858 Familistère
1898 Hellerau
1924 Haus Schröder
1928 Maison de Verre
1928 Villa Tugendhat
1928 Dessau-Törten
1945 Eames House
1947 Unité d'Habitation
1965 Metastadt
1969 Visiona 1
1970 Capsule Tower

1

1 In the 1930s, Kondratieff foresaw many major innovations and developments of the twentieth century.

The historical origins and subsequent development of the relevant disciplines we are concerned with here show as many violent contrasts as do the opinions of individuals. This refers not just to the subject matter taught, but above all to the theoretical and methodological positioning of architectural and design training compared to the classical natural sciences and humanities. In the context of worldwide ecological, economic, and social issues and challenges that are becoming ever more acute, the debate on the relevance of and need for research and increased understanding of architecture and urban planning, interior architecture, and design is one area that has become increasingly important.

Approaches to Research

"This follows the trend of design thinking in the twentieth century, for we have seen design grow from a trade activity to a segmented profession to a field for technical research and to what now should be recognized as a new liberal art of technological culture."

Richard Buchanan

For decades research in the area of architecture and urban planning was dominated by natural sciences, engineering, and the humanities. Projects and doctoral theses were concerned either with construction physics technology or with aesthetic priorities and the traditions of art, with each of these approaches pursuing its own methodology. With the emergence of interior architecture and design as disciplines in their own right, and with the transformations in society

Historical Development of Professions

Period	Arts and Crafts	Art + Sculpture	Architecture	(Civil) Engineering	Interior Design	Design
From 1700		1648 Académie royale de peinture et de sculpture, Paris 1667 Manufacture Nationale des Gobelins, Paris 1671 Académie royale d'architecture, Paris 1696 Kurfürstliche Akademie für Maler, Bildhauer, Architektur und Kunst, Berlin				
1700–1750				1747 Ecole Nationale des Ponts et Chaussees (ENPC), Paris		
1750–1800	1767 Ecole Royale Gratuite de Dessin, Paris 1776 Gewerbeschule, Hamburg	1761 Académie des Arts, Stuttgart 1797 Ecole nationales supérieures des Beaux Arts, 1797 Ecole spéciale de peinture, de sculpture et d'architecture, Paris		1794 Conservatoire National des Arts et Metiers (CNAM), Paris 1797 Ecole Polytechnique (X), Paris		
1799			1799 Bauakademie, Berlin			
1800–1850	1821 Gewerbeakademie, Berlin			1802 Militärakademie West Point 1829 Ecole Centrale Paris (ECP) des Arts et Manufactures		
1825			1825 Karlsruher Polytechnikum			
1846	1846 Staatliche Kunstgewerbeschule, Hamburg					
1855			1855-1870 Sempers Bauschule, Zürich	1855 Eidgenössisches Polytechnikum Zürich (ETH)		
1860–1907	1867 Kunstgewerbemuseum und –schule, Berlin 1877 Ecole Nationale des Arts Décoratifs, Paris (als Umstrukturierung der Ecole de peinture) Rhode Island School of Design (RISD), Providence 1896 Central School of Arts and Crafts, London		1879 Technische Hochschule Berlin		1904 Chase School, New York	
1907			Deutscher Werkbund (DWB), München			
1908	1908 Großherzogliche Sächsische Kunstgewerbeschule, Weimar (Vorläufer Bauhaus)					
1915			Design Industrial Association (DIA), London			
1919	1919 Staatliches Bauhaus, Weimar, 1925–33 in Dessau					1919 Staatliches Bauhaus, Weimar, 1925–33 in Dessau
1920–1950	1925 Ecole nationale supérieure des arts décoratifs, Paris (Ensad)				1920 New York School of Fine and Applied Art, 1949 Ensad, Paris	
1950–1970	Art Schools and Academies		1968 Ecoles nationales supérieures d'architecture (ENSA)		1954 Bund Deutscher Innenarchitekten in Detmold	1953 Hochschule für Gestaltung, Ulm (HfG) 1970 Hochschule für Gestaltung, Offenbach
1971 ff			Founding of Universities of Applied Sciences in Germany with the focus to applied education in natural sciences engineering and design			
2000 ff			Introduction of Bachelor and Master Programs (Master Researched Based)			

2

2 Historical development of training structures and academic disciplines in the fields of art, planning, and design.

that followed World War II, the focus increasingly began to shift to sociological, psychological, and economic issues and, from 1960 onward, this led to a discussion on methods, which also had an impact on the structure of the average training syllabus.

Inspired by Bauhaus ideas, the Hochschule für Gestaltung (HfG) Ulm, which was in existence between 1953 and 1968, became a place where problem formulations and the design process itself were considered systematically, thereby making a major contribution to establishing the discipline of design as an academic field [3] — especially as a large number of its lecturers and students subsequently took posts at institutions all over the world. The alumni of the Ulm School exerted the same kind of significant influence on design teaching worldwide that the Bauhaus students had exerted on architecture in the 1930s. Further development of these theoretical approaches was particularly marked in the USA and in Britain, where the universities were more firmly grounded in the classical sciences due to their proximity to the natural sciences, humanities, and engineering, than the academies of applied arts and sciences and art academies of the German-speaking world.

In the early 1960s Horst Rittel became one of the first people to examine the relationship between the classical sciences and design. In 1967 his work culminated in the publication of the *Design Methods Group (DMG) Newsletter* at the University of California in Berkeley. This publication's central assertion was that planning and design problems are, as Rittel puts it, "wicked problems" [4] — that is, their complexity is such that they cannot be solved solely with the standard

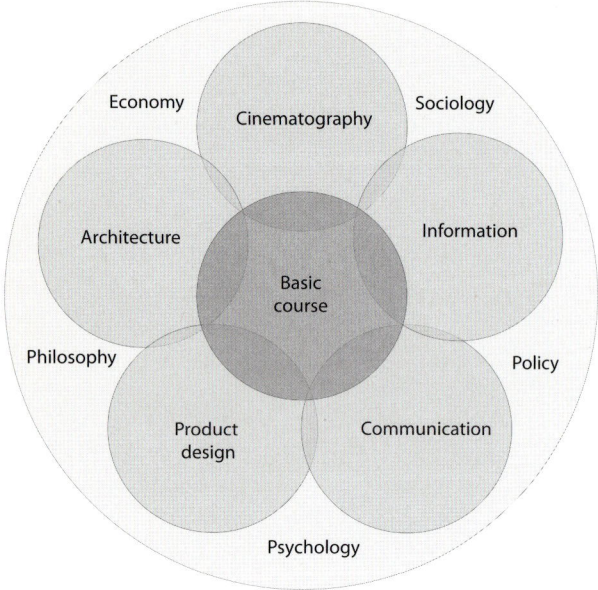

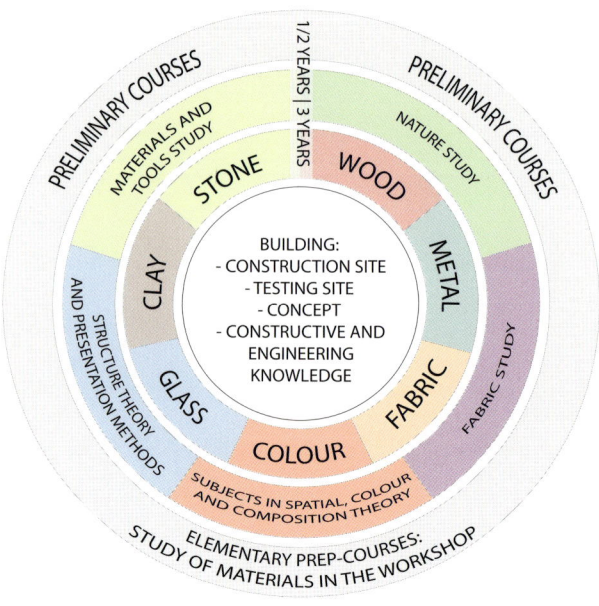

3, 4 The teaching curriculum at the HfG Ulm (3) was charaterized by a basic learning structure shared by all students, of the type that was also practiced at the Bauhaus Dessau (4). Building on this, students could specialize in various disciplines while incorporating the humanities and social sciences.

methods of classical science. At around the same time, Herbert E. Simon suggested that scientific methods should also be applied to the evaluation of man-made products (artifacts of design) [5]. L. Bruce Archer founded the Design Research Society in England in 1967, thereby bringing the term *design research* into use within the specialist community [6]. Previously, in 1964, Christopher Alexander had written the first Harvard dissertation on the subject of architecture that was concerned with the deconstruction of complex drafting problems into smaller units, which could then be solved by mathematics and logic. In the late 1970s, he developed a further method for tackling complex processes for which he coined the term *pattern language*. This method was also accessible to laypeople; it involved providing a collection of typical design models [7]. The term *design thinking* became widespread in the 1990s, becoming a standard concept worldwide due to its adoption by institutions and by research programs. This way of thinking was founded on interdisciplinary collaboration enabled by a shared system of values and methods understood by all parties, with a focus on creativity, teamwork, curiosity, a user-centered orientation, and a capacity for innovation [8].

It is becoming clear that the various branches of planning and design are developing more points of contact with one another in terms of theory and method, and are also increasingly interconnected with social and cultural sciences. The debate on the object and goals of planning and design research – a discipline that is still fighting for its place alongside established practices – is particularly marked in Europe. The process has been complicated by the fact that departments of interior architecture and design are generally affiliated to art institu-

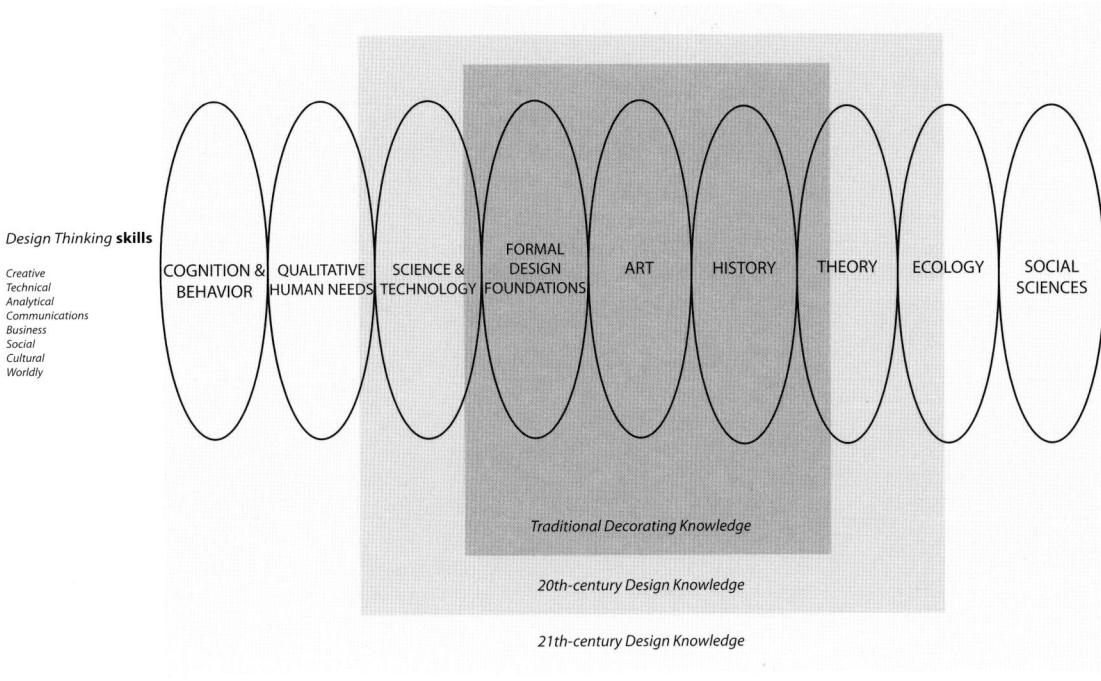

Design Thinking **skills**

Creative
Technical
Analytical
Communications
Business
Social
Cultural
Worldly

| COGNITION & BEHAVIOR | QUALITATIVE HUMAN NEEDS | SCIENCE & TECHNOLOGY | FORMAL DESIGN FOUNDATIONS | ART | HISTORY | THEORY | ECOLOGY | SOCIAL SCIENCES |

Traditional Decorating Knowledge

20th-century Design Knowledge

21th-century Design Knowledge

5

5 The increased construction density of cities and urban regions worldwide means a special responsibility for the design of the built environment in all fields of planning (taken from [8]).

tions or technical colleges, meaning that a culture of structured research has generally had to be built up from scratch. Recent publications in this field and a growing number of doctoral theses, however, show the discipline's increased scientific grounding [9]. Design research and design sciences are now on the way to becoming established in Germany and Europe as well. Ulrike Reichhardt believes that the reasons for this lie partly in a "lack of functional and emotional orientation" triggered by the current worldwide trend toward miniaturization (USBs instead of portfolios), automation (button presses instead of manual operation), and the abstract and ephemeral (cloud storage instead of a specific location) [10].

Human-Centered Design

"Design can and must become a way in which young people can participate in changing society."

Victor Papanek

Victor Papanek addressed these issues in 1971 in his book *Design for the Real World*, in which he offered guidance for "human ecology and social change" through the design of products and the environment [11]. In the introduction, he writes that: "As socially and morally involved designers, we must address ourselves to the needs of a world with its back to the wall ..." Now, forty years later, his words are being discussed with a new interest. In 1958, Charles and Ray Eames were invited by the Indian government to compile the India Report,

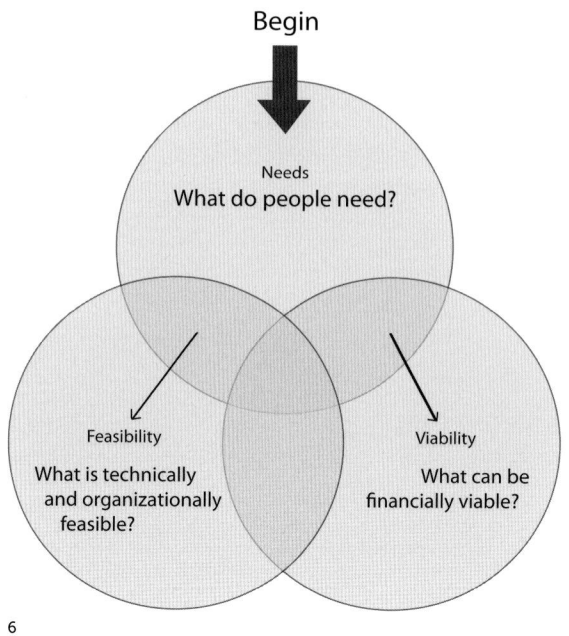

Begin

Needs
What do people need?

Feasibility

What is technically
and organizationally
feasible?

Viability

What can be
financially viable?

6

6 The firm IDEO has popularized
the human-centered design
method under the name Design
Thinking.

which contained recommendations for training in design. This led to the founding of the National Institute of Design (NID) in Ahmedabad, which saw itself as an institution whose "broadest service would in fact go to the people of India – [...] and through the fact that there was a group concerned solely with quality and performances of the things they, the people, used every day" [12].

In architecture, too, these experiments and discussions prepared the ground for the use of in-building technology – on the increase since 1960 – and the resulting "controllable interior climate," leading to increased and conscious discussion of interior comfort. Currently, the debate on the energy-efficiency of buildings, districts, and cities – necessitated by climate policy – and the requirements of demographic change are producing a great deal of discussion on the need for implementation to be as quick as possible, both in industrial nations and in emerging and developing nations. This situation is creating an increased awareness of the needs and actions of the user, which were previously taken into account during implementation only as peripheral factors – in spite of a growing number of people finding themselves using indoor spaces in a long-term or concentrated way due to their age or to the increased density of urban regions. It is obvious that the knowledge about the perception, impact, and use of spaces required for a human-centered design concept needs to be expanded and deepened [13].

In this case, *human-centered design* should be understood as an overarching term for further principles and methods, with the awareness that most terms in

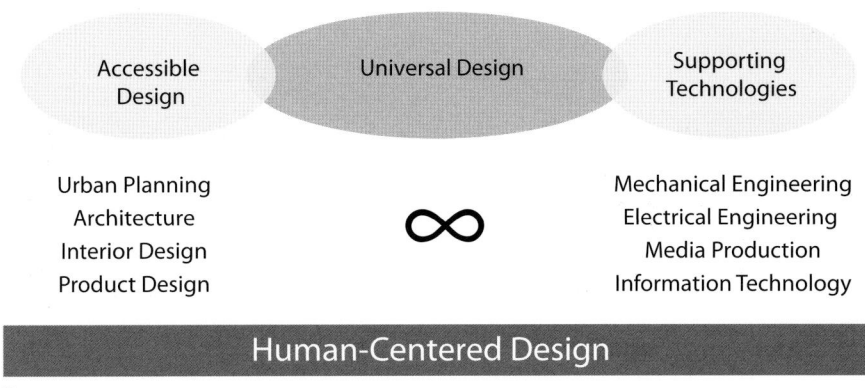

Accessible Design	Universal Design	Supporting Technologies
Urban Planning		Mechanical Engineering
Architecture	∞	Electrical Engineering
Interior Design		Media Production
Product Design		Information Technology

Human-Centered Design

7

7 *Human-Centered Design* should be understood as an overarching term for a number of methods that put human requirements at the center of the design and planning process.

general usage (English and German) are defined and used in different ways in American, Asian, and European cultural circles. These include:

> user-centered design (nutzerorientierte Gestaltung)
> barrier-free design, accessible design (Barrierefreiheit)
> design-for-all (Design für Alle)
> universal design, inclusive design (universelles Design)
> activity-centered design (handlungsorientierte Gestaltung)

While user-centered design focuses on the functionality of products and spaces for a particular target group, the other principles represent a more cross-target-group approach, emphasizing universal usability of products and spaces and aiming for extensive social involvement (inclusion). The objective of this unified approach is to improve day-to-day quality of life for all. The idea is not to design for a specific target or fringe group, but to enable usability for all – regardless of cultural heritage, gender, or physical and mental ability.

The expression *universal design* has now become established; its principles are becoming increasingly valid due to demographic change in industrial nations, with the emergence of a larger elderly and aging target group. At the Center for Universal Design at North Carolina State University, architects, researchers, product designers, and engineers have formulated the following principles of design:

1. Broad usability: the design should be usable by and marketable to people with a range of different abilities.

8

9

8 Many products of ambient assisted living (AAL) are heavily technology-driven and change the standard living environment considerably.

9 The evidence supports an approach that unites techno-logical aids with established technological applications and introduces them into the con-struction or spatial context.

2. Flexibility of use: support for individual preferences and possibilities.
3. Simple and intuitive functionality: readily comprehensible function regardless of the user's experience, knowledge, language capabilities, or current level of concentration.
4. Sensory information: the design should be effective in providing the necessary information, regardless of the environment and of the user's sensory capabilities.
5. Error tolerance: the design should minimize risks and the adverse effects of random or unintentional actions.
6. Low levels of physical exertion: the design should permit efficient and comfortable use with a minimum of fatigue.

In addition to this, research also focuses on ambient assisting technologies (AAT). This spectrum is wide, ranging from autonomous products such as spec-tacles and wheelchairs to space-specific concepts for working, living, and care spaces. These must be integrated into the space and the building's design. Of-ten, however, these projects and products are entirely market- or technology-based, and take little or no account of the specific details of individuals' lives. Robert Verganti comments that collaborations between engineers and the de-sign and planning professions to create user-centered design concepts is still not widespread – adding, provocatively, that this would appear to be the way forward for pioneering innovations [14]. Donald A. Norman spoke in a similarly critical vein in 2005, describing human-centered design as "detrimental" and instead advocating activity-centered design, which takes the sequence of hu-man actions as its starting point [15].

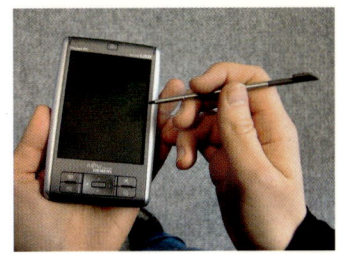

12

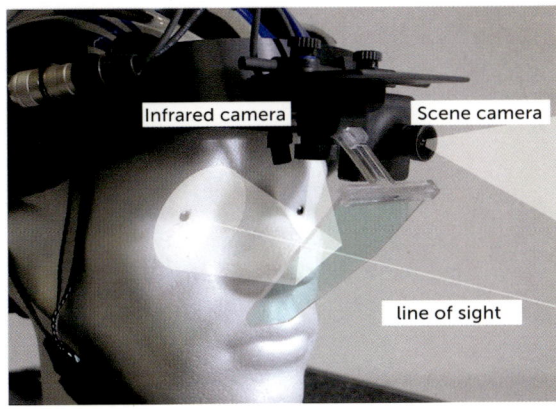

Infrared camera

Scene camera

line of sight

10

11

10 The mobile eye-tracking system can record the movements and gaze direction of the pupils.

11 It is used at the HS OWL primarily in orientation, with positive results.

12 Handheld devices support mobile data gathering onsite or in a variety of environments.

The integration of universally designed objects and technologies into spatial situations has previously been largely restricted to shapes – to the dimensions of components. The universal usability of rooms and buildings – in all respects, including atmosphere, emotional impact, and functionality – has previously received little attention. The planning disciplines are able to remedy this situation by bridging the gap between the different specialist fields involved, and refining product ideas by looking at rooms and buildings. Homes suitable for elderly people – placing a high value on homeliness, security, and identity – are one sector that has led the way in the integration of these disciplines. The challenge is to unite the required functional qualities with the required emotional qualities, both in rooms and in products; this calls for a high degree of flexibility and the incorporation of design that is suited to more than one phase of life. Ensuring the user's independence and autonomy in "normal" surroundings for as long as possible is an important factor, both emotionally and economically.

Architecture and Spatial Perception

"We make the impact of space measurable."

PerceptionLab

At the Detmold School of Architecture and Interior Design, there are two research departments concerned with technological and space design factors: the ConstructionLab and the PerceptionLab. While the ConstructionLab is primarily concerned with technological construction issues, the PerceptionLab focuses on analyzing a space's qualities, using real and virtual environments.

13

14

13 The real administrative space

14 The virtual administrative space

The aim of their research is to reach and to evaluate measurable and verifiable findings on the impact of perceptual qualities in architecture and spaces and to make these data available for the design and planning process [16]. The aim is to develop teaching and praxis toolkits using a variety of methods taken from natural sciences, humanities, and social sciences. Close links between the two departments are vital to refining products and methods. The following tools and methods are deployed:

1. Space laboratory: the implementation of room concepts on a 1:1 scale
2. Powerwall: virtual 3D scenes created by stereoscopic projection
3. Eye-tracking system: analysis and evaluation of visual perception
4. Biofeedback system: the recording of physiological data
5. Handheld devices and questionnaires: user surveys
6. Light laboratory: analysis and evaluation of illumination and lighting concepts

Using these methods, the two departments research a number of different goals and issues relating to the perception of space and architecture – incorporating, where possible, comparisons of real and virtual environments. Their investigations usually take place in the context of classes or as case studies, which are collaborations with external partners. Examples are [17]:

> Spatial experience: assessing the acceptance and usability of a space
> Test space: the effect of spatial surfaces in terms of well-being
> Digital material: developing a computer-based design tool for making a preliminary selection of atmosphere/design concepts

15

16

17

18

15 Martin Szeleky's glass stool is provocative because of its dimensions and solidity, as well as the use of glass for the seat. It causes us to question the way we usually experience materials.

16 A heating unit designed by Satyendra Pakhalé: an example of the adoption of regional design patterns taken from craft products for an industrial product as an expression of identity.

17 A sample of the real material was installed in one of the space laboratories and investigated using a number of methods.

18 The Powerwall simulation of real space is used primarily to investigate visual factors.

Spatial Experience: Acceptance and Usability

"A building as it is experienced is not a lifeless box. The inhabited space transcends the geometrical space."

Gaston Bachelard [18]

As with any optimization process, considering and documenting the precise reasons why projects have failed in order to learn from such failures – to discover the reason why, in spite of positive aspirations, the discussion and sharing of information between the planners and users did not produce the desired results – is vital to formulating principles for design and planning. What is required is a detailed analysis of user needs – functional and emotional – and, in second place, evaluation of actual use. In English-language planning and social sciences and building performance evaluation terminology, these two kinds of analysis are referred to as User Needs Analyses (UNA) and Post Occupancy Evaluation (POE). They draw on insights and methods from psychological and social sciences, which are always adapted to suit the specific situation. Methods taken from perception psychology that focus on identifying how individuals can be assisted in achieving their goals represent a further possible methodical approach that could usefully be deployed more often in practice.

In the Raumerlebnis (spatial experience) project, the real space (in this case, an administrative space) was compared with the virtual scenario, or "rendering." Observation, interviews, and questionnaires were deployed methodologically in

19

19–22 A number of visual scenarios show the different impact of different materials in the spatial context.

the real space. The eye-tracking system was also deployed as an aid to the "thinking aloud" method. In the virtual space, the emphasis was on visual perception, which was analyzed by comparing photographs with visualizations. Put together, the findings from all of these analyses (real and virtual) produced the following conclusions on how people perceived the corridor:

> The lack of color was perceived negatively – it gave the impression of grayness and monotony
> The planned expansion of the central hallway was viewed positively
> Openings and lines of sight into other rooms were evaluated positively
> The lack of interesting reference points in the hallway made orientation difficult

Test Space: Authenticity and Identification

"Appearance must carry a deeper, integrative argument about the nature of the artificial inhuman experience."

Richard Buchanan [19]

For large expanses of time – for whole epochs – architecture was dominated by a small number of locally available materials adapted to the climate or to local conditions. The specific use of materials in any given region – and thus the specific design of spaces – is therefore a concept that has developed over time, shaped by individual and cultural mentalities. A built environment, how-

20

ever, also expresses factors such as the need to impress, political power, and fashionable trends. In the age of globalization, a greater degree of material diversity, material transfer, and modification of conventional materials to suit a different cultural context have become the norm. An international construction industry has imposed this phenomenon on buildings of every kind, and is in the process of obliterating traditional craft processes. The sometimes inappropriate application of particular construction types – the most recent example of this being the popularity of fully glazed and therefore fully climate-controlled offices and residences in tropical and continental climates – is the expression of an extensively standardized planning and construction process and of expansionist marketing policy, often implemented without regard to the local climate and labor market. Ulrike Reichhardt views this as an opportunity for "designs, architecture, and plans developed by means of inclusive participation processes [...] to provide a counterbalance to globally oriented products, buildings, and regions by reinforcing cultural identities."

Planners and designers are now more aware of the importance of the acceptability and impact of the materials they use – of how they are perceived. User demand for appropriate designs and for a choice of surfaces adapted to individual requirements is on the increase, in both private and commercial contexts. The decorative surface is the interface where the first contact between the customer and the object takes place [20], and its aim is to produce particular emotions in the customers. The way a product is perceived changes constantly, as society's consensus on aesthetic standards shifts – and this is a phenomenon that relates to emotional criteria, rather than concrete product criteria. It was in

21

21 A realistic visualisation of materials with digital tools is important for the design process.

response to this that the research project Sensorische Gütebestimmung von Oberflächen (Sensory Classification of Surfaces) developed objective test procedures based on human perceptions and test panels [21].

The Proberaum, or test space project, looks at aspects of geometry, lighting moods, and materials by comparing a real test space with a virtual scenario. The stone veneer was installed in one of the space laboratories, where more than a hundred testers could touch and generally experience it.

Digital Material: Planning Tools

"Open innovation is a paradigm that assumes that firms can and should use external ideas as well as internal ideas, and internal and external paths to market, as the firms look to advance their technology."

Henry Chesbrough [22]

The Digital Material project involved making a comparative study of how different materials are perceived, in collaboration with a commercial company. The aim was to support the early stages of the design process by carrying out systematic modifications of surfaces and light situations in a number of virtual scenarios (renderings). The scenarios were also intended to provide realistic visualizations of the materials, in order to improve communication between the experts and the laypersons involved in the process (the architect and the client). Although those responsible for the design were primarily concerned with finding the visualization that was most realistic and the best in qualitative terms, this

22

analysis was also a way of considering and evaluating the impact of materials within a space. The renderings created for the project can be treated as an interactive materials library, facilitating quick comparison of digitized materials within the virtual space. This enables designers and users to use the renderings as a tool in the preliminary selection phase of the planning process.

Overview

The development processes, project and case studies presented here have contributed to an understanding of the impact of products, spaces, and buildings – on individual users, but also on larger groups. It has been understood ever since the beginnings of design and planning science that such an issue is a question of complex combinations, involving a number of different and overlapping levels of perception. Individual processes and methods will be defined and tested at a later stage, possibly through a combination of the principles of human-, user- and activity-centered design. Of more interest to us are the ways in which planners and designers can apply the available knowledge in energy-efficient or high-density construction – or construction suitable for elderly people – within specific nations and societies, in order to promote well-being and quality of life within a specific set of cultural and economic circumstances. This concerns the community's cultural construction consciousness as well, requiring the support of a wider public discussion and public education.

Digital Architecture:

From Design to Production

Marco Hemmerling
Ulrich Nether

New technologies effect changes in perception and thinking that are quite un-related to their actual content. They manufacture new realities. Or, as the Cana-dian media theorist Marshall McLuhan phrased it: "We shape our tools, and thereafter our tools shape us" [23]. McLuhan was expressing his belief that the development of media technologies is a trigger for social change. Digital con-tent influences the spaces in which we live, the objects with which we surround ourselves, the pictures we see, and the sounds we hear. Additionally, they define an expanded insight into, and sensitivity to, our reality. This development leads to a radical change in our environment — and, above all, creates an arena for design and for operation. In addition to fundamentally changing the working methods of architects and designers, the use of digital tools has fundamentally changed the process of formal design in the widest sense of the term — and consequently, the visual appearance of spaces and objects and how they are perceived. The computer software of today permits the generation of draft concepts that would previously have been hardly possible, either technologically or formally. By this token, computer technology has, to a great extent, divorced drafts from conven-tional production conditions. Issues now depend on digital rather than analog operations, in both the drafting process and production.

The computer abolishes the borders of imagination and permits operations that would previously have been made impractical by the limits to technology and time resources. The results of the fascinating possibilities of digital production, however, rarely get past a realm of formal experiments, which, in spite of their geometrical complexity, often appear shockingly one-dimensional. Greg Lynn, himself an exponent of free digital form worlds, stated his own critical opinion

1

1 Design for the SunSys pavilion
for the Campus Emilie, by Jens
Böke, Hochschule Ostwestfalen-
Lippe

of this condition of formal dependency ten years ago: "The computer brings with it a language of design in which one always begins by doing what the software does well" [24]. Computer-aided drafting and construction, however, could potentially benefit us far more than this quotation might lead one to believe. To unlock this potential, an understanding of the basic information technology resources made available by the computer is required. This kind of digital form development process achieves its results according to different principles – and is affected by different factors – from conventional processes. It is based on a new understanding of method – at the drafting stage and during the realization. But what is the profile of drafting in a digital age? What influence do these technologies have on architecture and design and on the role of future designers – and therefore on the teaching of draftsmanship today?

One self-evident observation is that the advent of information technology has led to a widening out of professional specialties: by being receptive to digital technology, architects and interior designers are able to open up interesting new areas of activity. In addition to changing drafting methods, these technologies allow the design abilities of an expert in spatial configurations to be extended to many areas of media and information technology, and of construction and production technology.

The impact on architecture of the use of digital media in the drafting and realization process is manifested in two strands of evolution. First, computers support the origination of concepts with the aid of digital tools. The comprehensive representation of three-dimensional design concepts by means of digital

2

2 SunSys, structural principle

simulations, with direct interaction with the virtual model enabled throughout the drafting process, significantly expands the perception of spatial and functional issues. Computer-generated representation, for instance, enables spatial concepts to be thoroughly reviewed, evaluated, and discussed at an early stage. Computers are now capable of representing the whole of the design and planning process, from the first digital draft to concept visualization to a complete 3D data set.

Second, the last few years in particular have seen a perceptible increase in computer-aided construction and production processes using CAD-CAM interfaces and rapid prototyping processes. One special feature of this technology is that a wide variety of forms can be produced using one and the same production process. As the working process is fully automated, the manufacturing price should, in theory, remain the same. Cost-related dependency on the standard product is thus largely avoided, introducing new design freedoms into architecture production. The manufacture of individual products using new production methods enables a project- and customer-specific end product, which has already become the established norm in some areas of production. A look at the major areas of use for digital tools demonstrates the extent and range of the influence exerted by computer-aided methods, even today – and especially in architecture production.

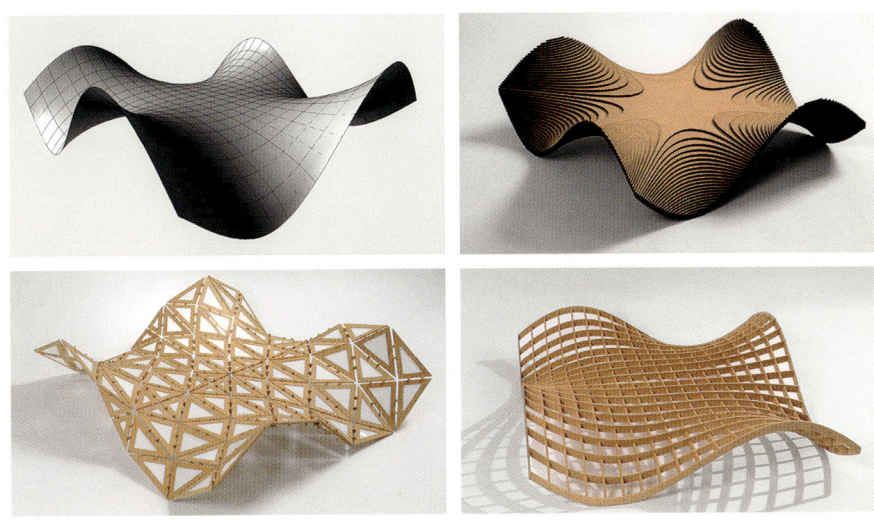

3

3 Construction variants for
translation surfaces, by
Frank Püchner, Hochschule
Ostwestfalen-Lippe

Digital Design

Drafting processes are characterized by an intuitive way of proceeding, which might appear difficult to reproduce when working on a computer. Very few architects and designers arrive at a draft concept by using the computer medium alone — although the computer can be seen replacing the pen in the early conceptual phase of drafting work among students and the younger generation of the profession in particular. The real potential of digital drafting, however, does not lie in simulating formerly analog operations, but in harnessing computer-immanent processes for data recording, compilation, data processing, and evaluation of complex interactions. This is a significant advance on classic CAD applications, which assist the drawing process but do not bring any new qualities to the drafting methodology.

Digital tools, on the other hand, make it possible to take new paths and to develop spatial and object concepts processually, based on a variety of parameters. The results are presented in real time, enabling a direct dialogue between the draftsperson and the draft [25]. This involves applying algorithms — a mathematical set of instructions — to the basis geometry, allowing the development of the forms to be influenced in a number of ways. Today, many software applications allow users to program their own scripts and algorithms by permitting the factors affecting the production of the draft to be individually defined. In other words, architects and designers can develop their own tools. This process-oriented procedure permits the overall structure to be manipulated in a manner that transcends scale within draft development, without losing the

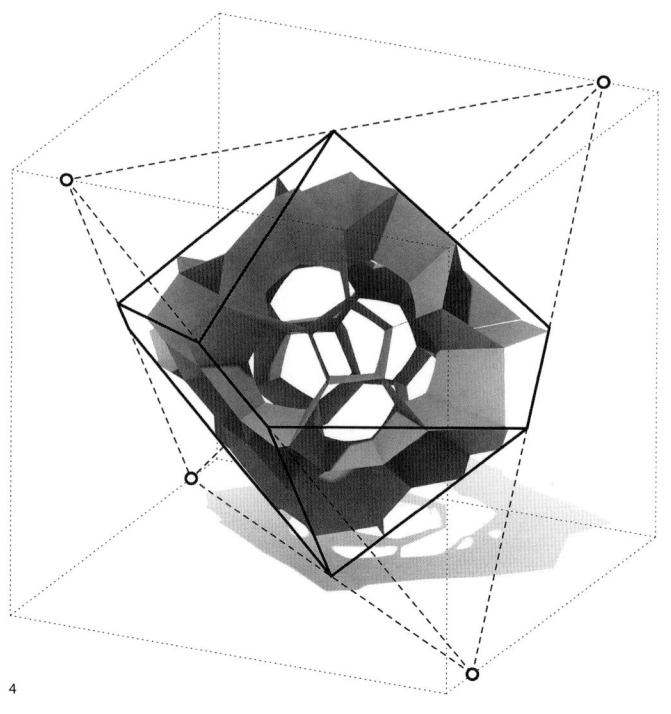

4

4 Parametric 3D model of the pavilion, Hochschule Ostwestfalen-Lippe

interconnections between the individual elements. In this process, the drafting activity is extensively supported by information technology, which permits what might be called an intuitive approach. To this extent, programmed parametric models encourage a new design method that requires knowledge of architecture, together with object-specific and computer-specific expertise.

In architecture, parametric models can be used to create structures that permit adaptation, and which can therefore respond to external influences such as exposure to sunlight and wind loads, or internal influences, such as user behavior and functional sequences. The architectonic form arises from the way in which individual parameters are connected and prioritized. Drafting is undergoing a shift from a formal graphic process to a strategic evolutionary process, with the designer drafting a system rather than a concrete result. One advantage of this approach – aside from making visible the dependencies in the design – is that it is flexible, allowing the designer to alter the programming at any time and therefore to quickly develop and evaluate different concepts or variations for a drafting solution. This makes spaces, in all their complexity, more accessible and controllable for the designer, something that also applies to the work of interior architects or designers.

Digital Production

Computer-aided production methods permit these digital 3D data to be translated into physical models or components. Digitally generated and machine-

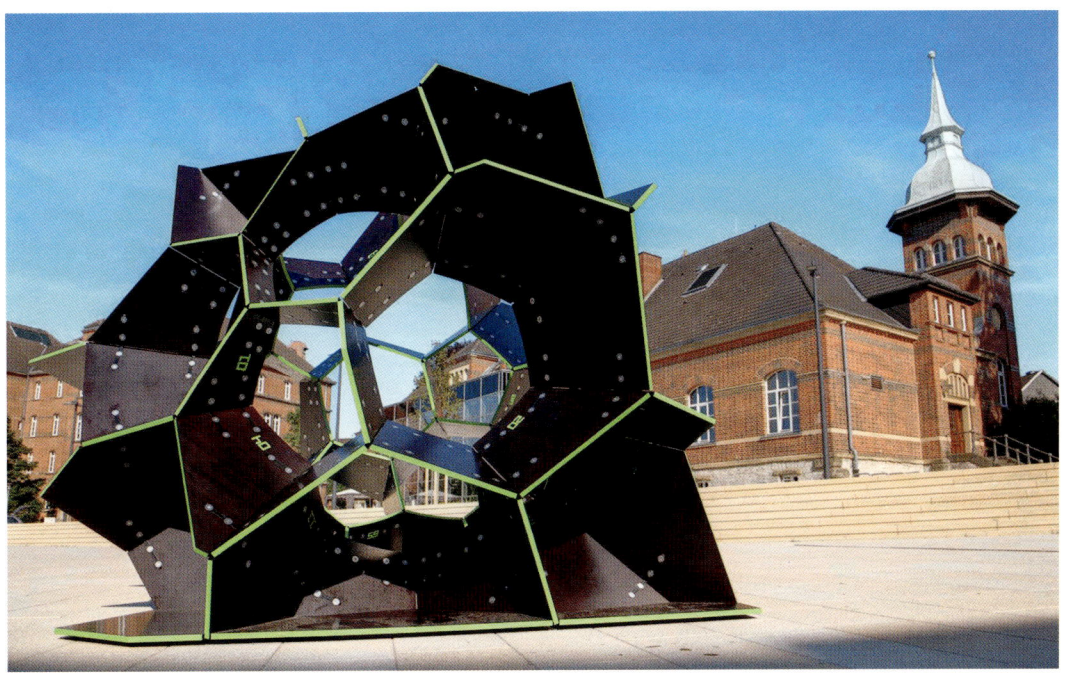

5

5 1:1 model of the pavilion

fabricated components expand the construction spectrum and incorporate the factors associated with materials decisions and manufacturing issues into the design process. Insights from the manufacturing process are fed back into the drafting process as programming parameters. These production methods, however, will not necessarily result in formal transformations in architecture. Instead, it is a question of applying methods in order to further refine and optimize processes. To this extent, digital fabrication methods are capable of more than simply creating individual structures with a higher degree of complexity. It is true that in comparison to other production areas, the construction implementation of architectural drafts is still largely based on traditional working processes. Whereas industrial production processes such as machine assemblage or the automotive industry produce highly developed technological products, buildings are almost always prototypes erected using traditional methods. In addition to being cost-intensive and time-intensive, the construction process fails to benefit from the design freedoms offered by digital draft development and computer-aided production. Developments in materials research and product technology lead in an entirely different direction.

As has been discussed, digital production has long become a major tool, if not the major tool, in industry. It is ubiquitous: no joinery workshop can be competitive without a CNC lathe, and no metalworking concern can be competitive without a computer-controlled hole punch or bending machine. For many years now, large-scale industry has used production sites where no human hand is involved in production. And yet drafting – which is a question of thinking in processes – continues to follow the same learned deterministic sequences.

At best, the computer's potential is employed to optimize use of materials or working patterns. As a rule, all the data that are fed into the computer derive from our experiences and traditions in dealing with the things and the processes that led to its manufacture.

The more the desired result is, by necessity, dictated by individual requirements, the more digital processes will be integrated into the whole sequence of development and production. Two examples that concern us very directly are replacement teeth and prosthetic limbs: once manufactured in a painstaking manual process requiring a large number of modifications and adaptations, today they are frequently created by means of harmonized digital processes, from measuring procedures to completion. In spite of a relatively high initial investment, we are seeing these processes become more established over time.

The sectors in which the "rapid process" has become the norm are generally those in which speedy completion is a priority – the production of product components for product development projects, for instance, or racing car design. This allows the processes to be improved by digital methods while also improving the functionality and ease of use of the products themselves, complete with optimization of materials selection and design. Experts in process technology engineering are predicting a breakthrough into mainstream industry in the coming years.

In the foreseeable future, we can therefore expect the computer to become the tool that guides industrial design, from the initial idea to the completed product, translating virtual formulations directly into realities – and thereby responsible for creating the things that surround us in our day-to-day lives.

This will introduce a new quality to mass customization – instead of simply being able to choose between a number of colors and upholsteries, we will be able to acquire products that are suited to our needs in terms of function, form, size, and material. And because we will want to possess these individually tailored objects, the world of production and design will change. Coupled with developments in media and lighting technology, this new state of affairs might, for instance, create the following scenario:

"It is possible that in twenty years' time, we will be printing out shoes precisely suited to our anatomical and aesthetic requirements at home in our workrooms, and doing the same thing in the kitchen to produce our favorite vine-ripened tomatoes, all the while sitting back in our armchairs – which will, of course, be precisely tailored to our needs – in living rooms which, when we turn on the TV, become stages upon which virtual characters move in three-dimensional space" [26].

Digital design and production will make it possible to combine industrial production with individually tailored items. This development also offers us the possibility of being able to relate to objects again in the way that we once related to manually produced objects – something that has been lost to us in everyday life in a culture of industrial mass-production – thereby restoring to objects their true value. This paradigm shift and the resulting changes in method will need designers and implementers with a philosophy that places the emphasis on certain qualities. It will not be a question of generating a "brave new world" with more complex, seemingly fantastical designs, but of marrying the seemingly inexhaustible possibilities of parametrically developed design to a sense of responsibility and avoidance of excess.

This responsibility on the part of the designer is not restricted to the process of turning a digital product into a tangible product – the tangible object itself will increasingly be changed as projection of the digital becomes a reality. Interaction, communication, and utility are coming increasingly to the fore, as the objects themselves become increasingly subordinated to the effect that they achieve. In this way, spaces and objects derived from digital processes will, in the best outcome, develop a self-sufficient quality founded on user-orientation and adaptivity, suitability of materials and production technique, and effective sustainability. In this last respect, nature can be said to parallel the options for drafting and manufacture that we have identified.

Digital Sustainability

"Perfection is not attained when there is nothing more that can be added, but when there is nothing more that can be taken away" [27]. Notwithstanding the apparent contradiction contained in its diversity, nature is structured so that it constantly fulfills this condition. Optimization is essentially a never-ending stage-by-stage selection process. This is precisely what the digital process makes possible. It is also the next challenge for architecture and design: how can a state of progressive constant improvement – an evolutionary progression – be introduced into all processes? If we extend this thought, we arrive at a cycle comparable with the cycle of nature – a state of true sustainability. This involves developing materials and processes that approximate nature and its principles. Ultimately, by transcending user-orientation and replacing it with affordance – of the kind that we see in the natural world and its self-sufficient complexities – we obtain the key to defining an aesthetic and the way forward for a new unity of nature and design.

Currently, we feed data into the computers, defining the extent of the research and defining the fundamentals, the idea and concept. In the future, the machines will be able to learn for themselves, enabling them or their operational arms autonomously to find the best ways of creating the right form for a concept, to make an informed decision. The aim of the postgraduate master's degree study program in computational design and construction at the Detmold School of Architecture and Interior Design, based at the Hochschule Ostwestfalen-Lippe, is to make use of the considerable potential inherent in these developments. It is based upon a professional profile that unites digital drafting and production methods to create an overall perspective. This means that in addition to relevant specialist architecture and interior design subject matter, the syllabus includes basic informational science and computer-aided production. One significant factor in the complexity of the planning process is the number of requirements relating to the various specialist disciplines, which must be integrated as one progresses from drafting to realization. This calls for design, planning, technological, organizational, and communication skills on the part of the planners. Classes place a particular emphasis on the interfaces between the various disciplines and phases of planning. This is partly in response to the increasing demand for graduates with good qualifications in the interdisciplinary field, who can bring together information technology, architecture, and design [28].

But how can these various methods be harnessed for the development of sustainable architecture and space design? And, working in this way, how can an autonomous means of expression be defined that satisfies current and future demands?

One significant advantage of using computer-aided methods is that they offer a variety of possibilities for strategically combining the individual processes, exploiting synergies and recognizing problems at an early stage and developing strategies to circumvent them. A process-oriented approach of this kind is founded on the development of a consistent and adaptable drafting model that can be refined in design terms and successively expanded and supplemented by adding new information as the planning progresses. The end result of this process is an integrative architecture based on the interaction of various factors, such as a space's impact and the form, materials, construction, and production conditions, together with user behavior, sustainability criteria, and budget issues.

Digital drafting creates a direct connection between possibilities of thought and possible constructions. To this extent, the computer has developed from being purely a drawing instrument that simply simulates traditional instruments to become an integrative drafting medium with its own special qualities and requirements. The computer is surely the most all-embracing and dynamic medium that has ever been available to a working designer. In order to develop this potential fully, however, we must be able to deploy the computer as an interactive instrument and see its artificial intelligence as permitting the expansion of creativity. The challenge that faces us is that of fulfilling this role for our information society and of creating the rooms of the future by becoming more proficient in dealing with digital media.

The initial reality of the physical space and the virtual reality of digitally generated environments are increasingly coming together to create an emergent single experience. The arena in which we can act is expanding and the design instruments at our disposal are becoming more diverse. Above all, they are creating a connection between the two worlds [29]. Hani Rashid, cofounder of the New York architecture firm Asymptote, describes this augmented reality design field as follows: "We will continue to see experiments with the virtual that leave the confines of the screen, and merge the virtual with the real, spaces that will ultimately blur the distinctions of what we currently think constitutes a real experience versus a virtual experience" [30]. It will become increasingly difficult to draw a clear line between the two. Just as our consciousness collates individual experiences in order to form an overall picture, we will arrive at a point where we think of elements from physical and virtual life simultaneously, and design them simultaneously. This kind of emergence is a question of uniting different factors to create a quality of the new type of space. This is a task that is a natural part of the profession of architects and interior designers – professions that involve the interfacing of people, spaces, and objects.

Facade Road Map: Paths and Pathfinders

Ulrich Knaack

Vision

In pronouncements about new developments and/or products, the word *innovation* is understood to mean "anything new." More properly, however, an innovation is a new idea or invention, a new product on the market, a new economic strategy, or a successful new functional application [31]. Our subject here is innovation in construction, which covers both actual products of construction and the circumstances that led to their development, and also covers potential ways forward that may hold the key to further developments and to future actual projects.

Method

In order to arrive at an understanding of the development of facades, the author, working in association with the ConstructionLab at the Hochschule Ostwestfalen-Lippe (HS OWL) and the Facade Research Group at the TU Delft, has developed a facade "road map," which covers the full timescale of building envelope development – from the massive wall to the elementarized, free-form aluminum facade – and distinguishes between massive and framework structures (monolithic buildings on the one hand and frame-built buildings on the other are understood to represent the principal construction types) [32]. The timescale is logarithmically tapered in relation to the current date – because one's own area of focus, and therefore the best state of understanding, is always located in the current moment, and because the development frequency of

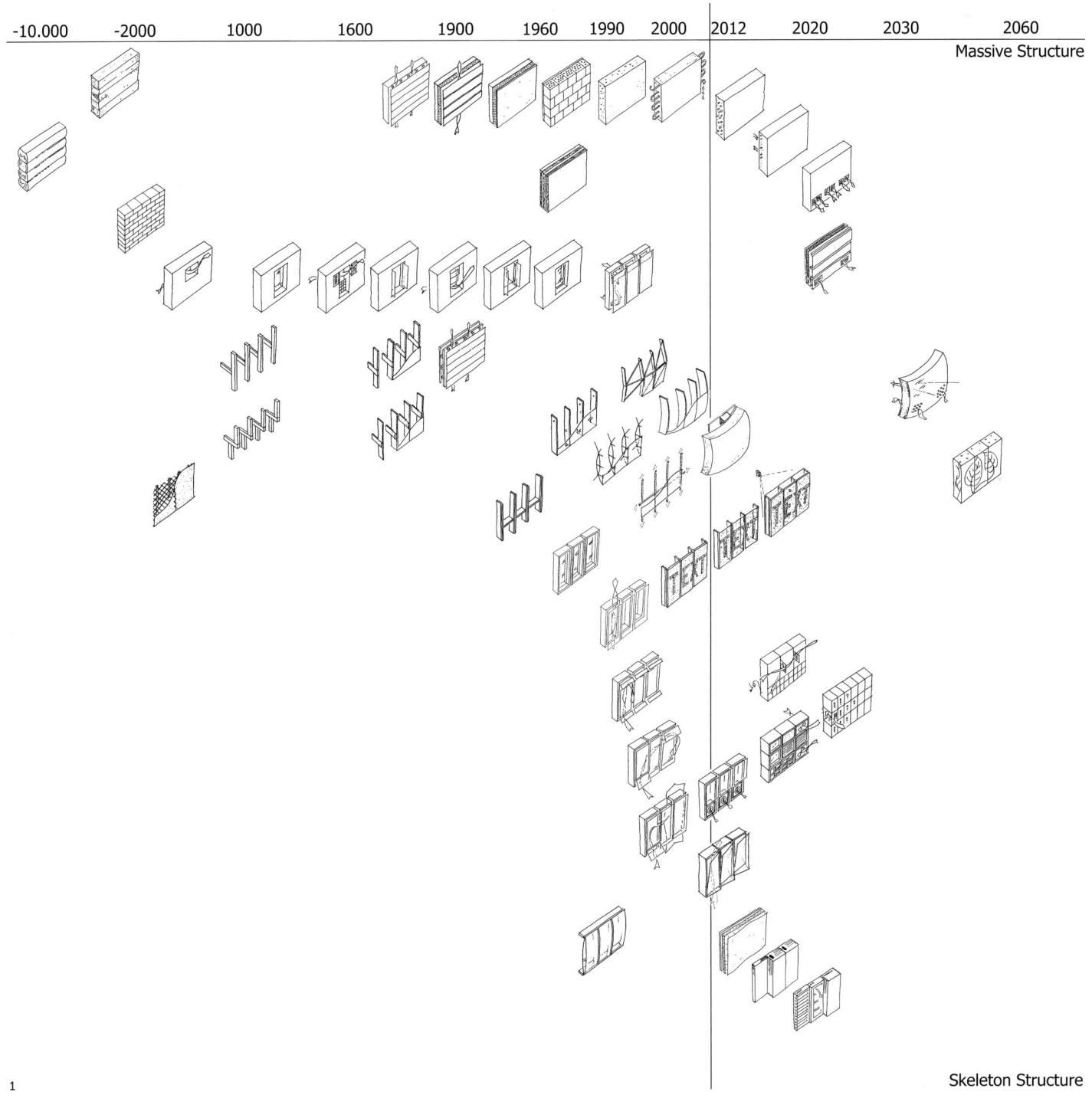

Massive Structure

Skeleton Structure

1

1 Facade Road Map

2

2a

3

2 Royal Botanic Garden in Kew
(Richard Turner, Decimus Burton,
1844–48)

2a Kibbel Palace (John Kibbel,
1873)

3 Lattice shell, Museum of
Hamburg History (Volkwin Marg
+ Jörg Schlaich, 1989)

technical innovations increases exponentially [33]. This results in a map that shows the individual stages of development as a technical evolution process, detailing the succession of functional requirements and the resulting practical applications of the technology. In order to make this development visible, the schema goes on to detail five identifiable isolated development cycles. The explanatory information focuses on functional and constructive parameters and on the people responsible for initiating developments.

From the greenhouses of the nineteenth century to the glazed lattice shell

I begin with the glass constructions of the nineteenth century, as this is an area in which isolated parallel developments in facade developments can easily be identified. In the first third of the nineteenth century, the need to protect plants brought from colonial territories against the English climate while still putting them on display resulted in an era of increasingly delicate British glasshouses. John Claudius Loudon (1783–1843) could be described as the first notable creator of such structures, although he was in fact a landscape gardener by profession. Loudon's early experience with lean-to greenhouses led him to develop the ridge-and-furrow roof, which will be explained further at a later stage. He also developed and implemented lattice shells constructed from cast-iron rods, which were parabolic in order to ensure the optimal orientation in relation to the sun. The small-format glass panes used in these constructions gave the shell additional rigidity as well as sealing off the interior.

4

5

6

4 Lattice shell, hippopotamus house, Zoological Garden, Berlin, with exposed termination of edge (J. Gribl + Schlaich Bergermann und Partner – 1997)

5 Junction solution, hippopotamus house, Zoological Garden, Berlin

6 Lattice shell, British Museum, London (Norman Foster + Buro Happold, 2000)

Loudon was succeeded by Joseph Paxton (1801–1865), who shared the same background in landscape gardening. He deployed the ridge-and-furrow roof – in the form of mutually supporting glass panes, similar to a truss construction – for the Crystal Palace, built to host the Great Exhibition of 1851. Aside from the technical finesse of its construction, its dimensions, and logistical implementation, this project is significant because it led to glass being seen as an acceptable material for public and pleasure buildings. John Kibbel's (1815–1894) Kibbel Palace (1873) is our final example of glass construction from this period: originally a watchmaker, Kibbel used cast-iron lattice shells, which operated as a shell only once the glass had been installed [34].

The era of the lattice shell began a good hundred years later, with the courtyard roof of the Museum of Hamburg History (1989). This generation of lattice shells consist of a bar grid prestressed by a diagonal cable net to stabilize it against asymmetrical loads. The space within is enclosed by panes of glass, although these are not part of the load-bearing system. Aside from the precision of the shapes involved, junction geometry was a significant factor. The emergence of a variety of different junction types – from simple cuts to free-form milled parts – kept pace with advancements in production technology. At this stage, development was driven by the desire for the construction to be kept as delicate as possible and by technical advancements in glass manufacture and geometrical aspects of fabrication as well as unconventional approaches by those responsible for the constructions [34].

7

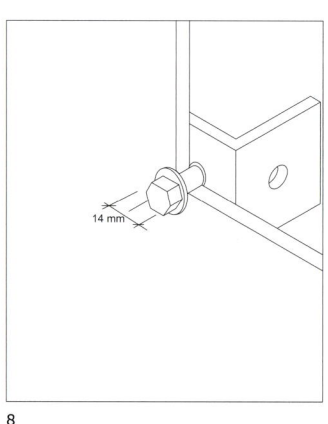

8

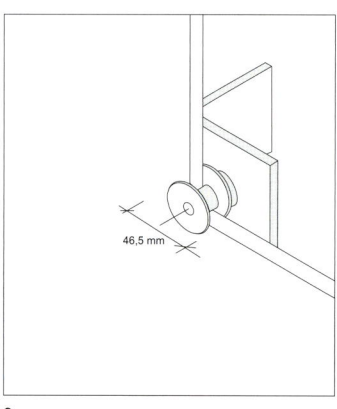

9

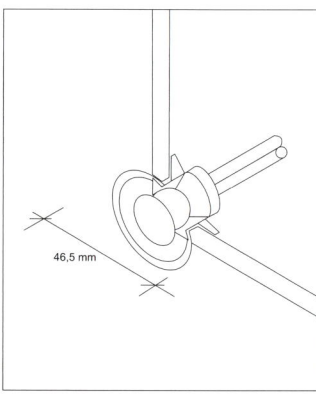

10

7 Renault UK's Parts Distribution Centre in Swindon (Norman Foster, 1982)

8 Patch fitting

9 Planar fitting

10 Hinged fitting

11   12

11 Glazed garden at the
technology museum Cité des
Sciènces et de l'Industrie –
Parc de la Villette (Peter Rice,
1986)

12 Nederlands Architectuurinstituut Rotterdam (Jo Coenen,
Mick Eekhout, 1993)

The change from drilling to flexible mounting of glass in the late twentieth century

Due to the desire to make the construction as delicate as possible and to achieve maximum transparency – and in spite of production and construction constraints that limited the maximum size of glass elements – this epoch saw numerous efforts by architects and construction designers to develop alternative glass-mounting systems. In 1982 Norman Foster developed a glass mounting system that sat atop a post-and-beam system for Renault UK's Parts Distribution Centre in Swindon. He used glass panes that were drilled and held in place by means of bolts or "patch fittings." The aim was to dissociate the glass from the substructure in order to bring a high degree of transparency into the design. In 1986 this development was taken a step further by Peter Rice (1935–1992) in the glazed garden at the technology museum Cité des Sciènces et de l'Industrie – Parc de la Villette. Rice realized that the process of drilling a brittle material like glass and fixing it so as to ensure flexural stability restricted load application and deformation options for facades, and therefore developed a solution that involved flexible point fastenings. The fastenings were positioned so that the lines of force intersected in the joint, thereby avoiding flexural loads on the mounts. The foyer area of the Nederlands Architectuurinstituut in Rotterdam – created in 1993 by Jo Coenen with a construction solution by Mick Eekhout – was one of the first buildings to use this fastening principle for insulating glass panes. The inner panes were drilled, and the outer panes were held in place by adhesive edge seals, satisfying the requirements for good thermal properties in a fully glazed facade [4]. The new technology used for drilling the

13

14

13 Cable net facade, Eissport-
halle Olympiapark, Munich
(Kurt Ackermann, with Jörg
Schlaich, 1983)

14 Cable net facade of the
Kempinski Hotel, Munich Airport
(Murphy / Jahn, with Jörg
Schlaich, 1993)

glass panes was innovative, as was the rigorous adherence to standards and the understanding of force flow in the glass panes. These developments were pushed forward by architects, by construction designers, and by those responsible for manufacturing the material and for executing the construction work [34].

Cable net facades

For the Eissporthalle Olympiapark project in Munich, Jörg Schlaich collaborated with Kurt Ackermann to develop an even, vertically prestressed cable system, with the aim of further minimizing the load-bearing structure contained in the glazed building envelope. Due to a combination of short distances and the prestressing forces, this system was subject to virtually no deformation. The glass panes could be held in place by clamp mounts to form an enclosure for the interior space. Working on the Murphy / Jahn Kempinski Hotel (at Munich airport) project of 1993, Jörg Schlaich used the same principle in developing a level cable net, which, at maximum wind load, registered a deformation of up to 1/25 and was therefore able to transmit forces as necessary. One consequence was that the glass panes had to be elastically mounted to avoid their being subjected to heightened flexural loads at the corners as the system deformed. Rijk Rietveld and Mick Eekhout developed a cable net that incorporated glass fiber cables built into the panes of insulating glass, based on a concept by the author. The aim of this system – used for the Inholland University of Applied Sciences project in Delft in 2010 – was to cut down further on the visible elements.

15

15 Glass fiber cable-net facade,
Inholland University of Applied
Sciences, Delft (Rijk Rietveld,
with Mick Eekhout, 2010)

16

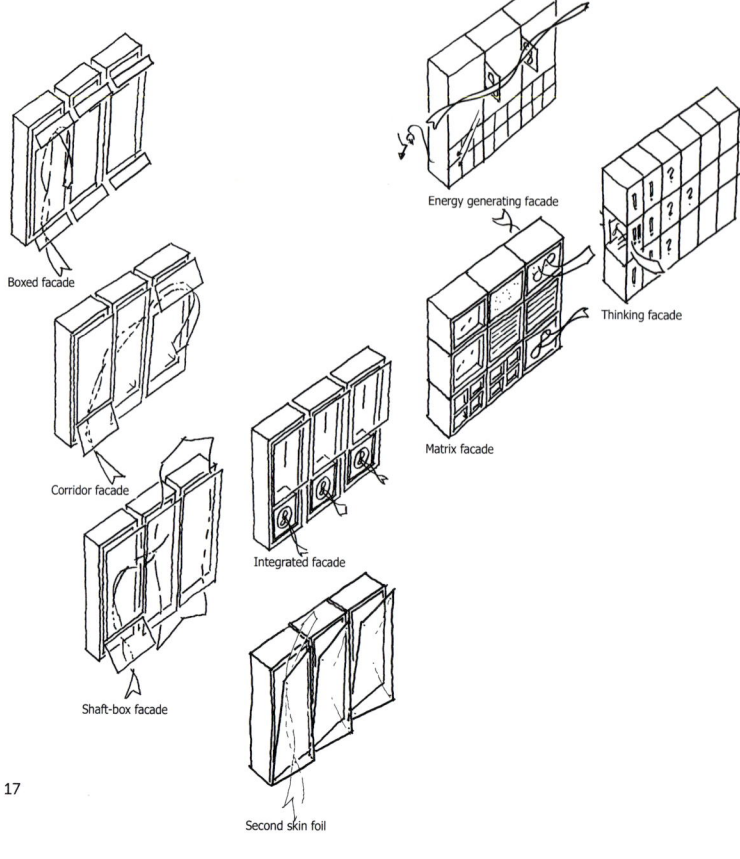

Boxed facade

Corridor facade

Shaft-box facade

Integrated facade

Second skin foil

Energy generating facade

Thinking facade

Matrix facade

17

16 Lloyd's of London
(Richard Rogers, 1986)

17 Facade road map with
double facades as the focus

This new phase in the evolution of glass systems also owed its development to construction designers who were able to count on architects to accept new ideas and on those responsible for implementing the concept to be creative and to take risks [34].

Double facades and component facades

Energy consumption issues are a counterbalance to the desire for an open and transparent building envelope. This aspect of the building envelope was brought into sharp focus by the oil crisis of 1973: the glazing insulation values of the time were unsatisfactory, resulting in high energy consumption values for any building that incorporated large expanses of glass. In the late twentieth century, the newly open and democratic nature of society expressed itself in a desire for open buildings [35], which involved large-format glass surfaces. The need to take account of the energy-related properties of these surfaces produced a generation of facades that took on the role of conditioning the climate within the building as well as enclosing and sealing off the interior space [36].

This cycle began with Richard Rogers's 1986 Lloyd's of London project. Here, Mike Davies, working for Rogers's firm, developed the "polyvalent wall" – a single multilayered element intended to supply all facade functions while conserving the required amount of energy. As the technology required to realize this vision was as yet unavailable, an alternative facade solution for the building was developed. In line with the "high-tech architecture" dictates of the time, the technological components were positioned toward the outside of the building,

18

19

20

21

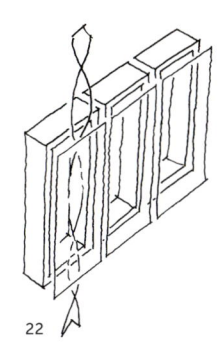

22

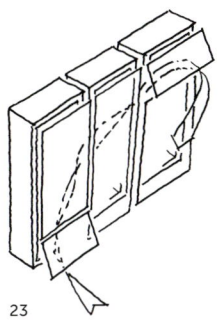

23

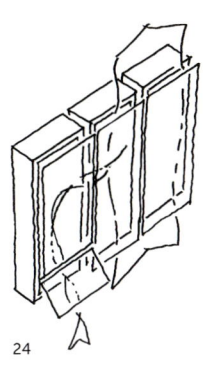

24

18 Box window and double skin facade

19 Shaft-box facade, ARAG Düsseldorf (Foster + Partners, with RKW Rhode Kellermann Wawrowsky, 2000)

20 Corridor facade of Stadttor Düsseldorf (Petzinka Pink und Partner, 1998)

21 Box window

22 Double skin facade

23 Corridor facade

24 Shaft-box facade

with the ventilation and exhaust conduits and the transparent and opaque areas clearly visible. Proposals for incorporating additional functions, which were drawn up for this project but never implemented, played a significant role in subsequent developments. A generation of double-shelled glass facades – known as double facades – emerged. This facade form can be divided into a number of categories, but all variants incorporate an additional air-filled intermediate space that acts as a climatic buffer. This layer is transparent. It provides wind and sun protection and facilitates natural ventilation.

From a structural point of view, the *box window facade* must be considered to be the simplest solution. It involves sealing off individual windows by means of a second layer of glass on their outer side. The *double-skin facade* places a second facade of glass around the whole building, which extends across the building's full height. Alternatively, stories can be separated in functional terms by means of a *corridor facade*. The *shaft-box facade* was developed to improve control of the functioning of the buffer zones between the levels. It consists of a combination of box windows and a vertical arrangement of glass shafts, which facilitate ventilation and exhaust processes by harnessing thermal lift [36, 37].

The next step in this development, the *component facade*, incorporates active in-building system components (concerned with ventilation and lighting) traditionally housed within the building itself. Helmut Jahn's 2003 Post Tower in Bonn can be regarded as the starting point for this development. Climate engineers from the firm Transsolar added in-house systems to the component facade concept by integrating climate control devices into the roof's face. The

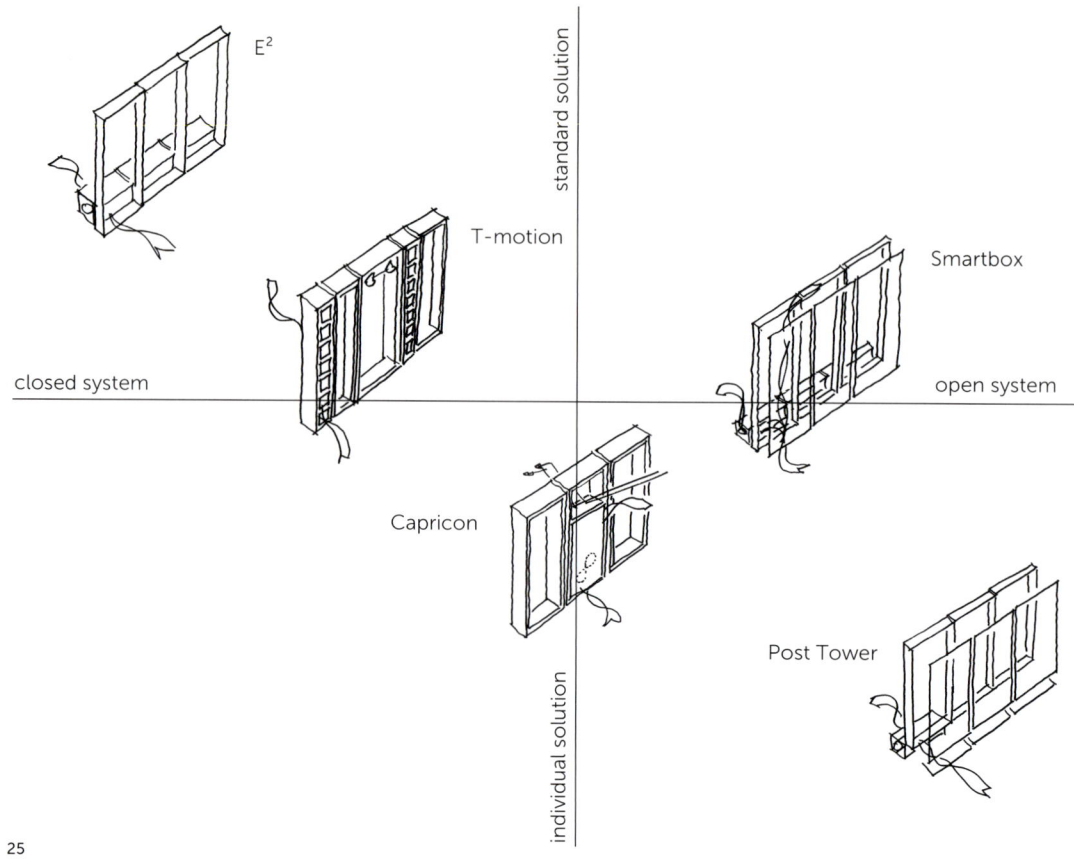

E²

standard solution

T-motion

Smartbox

closed system

open system

Capricon

individual solution

Post Tower

25

26

27

28

25 An overview of component facades and their spectrum of application

26 Post Tower, Bonn (Helmut Jahn with Transsolar, 2003)

27 Post Tower, Bonn, detail solution for integrating in-building systems components into the facade

28 Prototype T-Motion facade by Wicona

29

30

29 Capricorn Haus, Düsseldorf
(Gatermann und Schossig, 2006)

30 Capricorn Haus, Düsseldorf:
detail solution for the modular-
ized in-building system components

next stage arrived with the T-Motion concept study by the facade manufacturers Wicona, which, in addition to including previously integrated functions, incorporated artificial lighting into the space between the panes. Similar concept
solutions are present in the Smartbox by Cepezed / Delft and in the E²-facade
by the facade manufacturer Schüco. In 2006 the Capricorn project in Düsseldorf by Gatermann + Schossig included a successful integration of artificial
lighting of this kind.

It is interesting to note that this phase in the development of building shells was
driven forward by architects who, with the support of climate engineers, took
the risk of developing new systems for projects that were large enough to justify such a step, and were supported by the component and facade manufacturers in the second phase. Analysis of this situation shows that the approaches
taken by architects consistently produce individualized solutions, whereas solutions developed by companies are standardized and less flexible due to the
need for broad applicability. This analysis distinguishes the capability for integrating components that are not part of the original system and the standardi-
zation of system solutions [34, 39].

The NEXT facade was developed in collaboration between Kawneer Alcoa,
TROX, Somfy, Cepezed, and the TU Delft, based on an analysis of the limitations
of system-oriented component facades. In addition to an aluminum load-bearing system and the in-system media provision, it enabled additional in-building
system components to be integrated, making it an open system. In a further
project, the facade planning firm ImagineEnvelope, The Hague, developed the

31

32

33

31 NEXT facade. An open-system component facade.

32 Fully openable Solarlux Co2mfort facade in Nijverdal

33 Ekris Headlights in Utrecht (Kas Oosterhuis, 2007)

"Co2mfort facade" for the Solarlux company, to be used for that company's own new premises in Nijverdal in the Netherlands. In addition to the standard solutions, this corridor facade system enabled the facade to be entirely opened up, avoiding excessive heat during the summer while ensuring maximum transparency. Both of these are examples of an existing system being further refined through cooperation between planners and operators involving an open research and development approach.

Freeform facades

Fundamentally, the development of construction systems goes hand in hand with the development of manufacturing technologies. The same is true of the development of planning instruments, especially when the planning and the production are, ultimately, building upon the same basis – the same data sets. This becomes apparent when one reviews the evolution of digital planning instruments: the development of FEM in the 1940s, the first CNC processes in the 1950s, software and hardware development in the 1980s, and CAM and 3D modeling systems in the 1990s [39]. This background knowledge makes the development described below more easy to read, enabling us to recognize the evolution of formal principles in terms of design geometry – although not in terms of structural engineering's impact on forms and shapes.

The Utrecht Ekris Headlights project of 2007, by Kas Oosterhuis, is a suitable starting point for an outline of technical development, chiefly because of the choice of junction system: a steel tubing system composed of triangles based

34

35

34 Guggenheim Museum in
Bilbao (Frank O. Gehry, 1997)

35 Detail solution for Guggenheim Museum in Bilbao

on the free-form principle. In the junction areas, the glass layer is held in place by means of a separate profile system, with the separation facilitated by spacers. This achieves a separation of the load-bearing construction and of the building envelope.

Frank O. Gehry's Bilbao Guggenheim Museum of 1997 makes use of a similar system, with the load-bearing structure system separated into a number of layers in order to create the building's forms: on a steel main system is mounted a secondary load-bearing system, also steel, and onto this is mounted a load-bearing system for the free-form envelope. A further refinement – also by Frank O. Gehry – can be seen in the Walt Disney Concert Hall in Los Angeles, built in 2003: here, two further steel sub-load-bearing structures are fitted in addition to the main steel load-bearing structure, with the support structure for the free-form outer shell secured to one of them by means of adjustable fine-detail elements. This allows the form of the building to be more easily created and for it to be better adapted to local conditions.

The highly complex Kunsthaus Graz design by Peter Cook, from 2003, presents us with the most ambitious solution of any project within this cycle. For the Kunsthaus, in addition to a main system and a steel sub-load-bearing structure, Cook developed a covering system that used sheet metal panels, with a waterproofing layer lying atop it and, mounted atop the waterproofing layer, a cladding layer composed of backlit polycarbonate. In particular, the design's geometrical conception and the transition from the triangle-based geometry of the main load-bearing structure to the (quadratic) geometry of the cladding posed

36

37

36 Walt Disney Concert Hall in
Los Angeles (Frank O. Gehry,
2003)

37 Detail solution for
Walt Disney Concert Hall in
Los Angeles

compatibility problems during planning and production, and impacted on the parameters for the dimensions of construction components.

One striking observation that can be gained from the development described here is that once a possibility for developing a design for free-form architecture has been recognized in principle, the difficulty lies in translating it into a practicable construction. Architects could be said to be the driving force behind further refinements, but such refinements can only be implemented where operational software and suitably skilled construction designers and firms exist to carry out the implementation. A generation of 3D specialists can be seen emerging in all groups involved in the construction process.

Innovation?

As was remarked at the outset, an innovation – in the true sense of the word – is a new idea or invention, a new product on the market, a new economic strategy or a successful new functional application [31]. From this, we can see that innovation in construction is never created by the unilateral activities of a single party – it is always an interplay involving a number of different parties:

> The architect / designer, who, in his or her search for something that does not yet exist, takes on board formal aspects and creates a new formal configuration

38

38 Kunsthaus, Graz (Peter Cook, 2003)

> The construction designer, who, with the aim of doing something new, introduces new technical possibilities into construction, plugs any gaps in the design's performance, or comes up with appropriate compromises

> The system manufacturers and/or construction implementers, who, based on the requirements imposed by the projects, must ultimately make the construction feasible

One interesting conclusion that can be drawn from all our observations is that developments ultimately derive from individuals and their motivation, or even from blind coincidence – at any rate, construction developments are never due to the systematic process of searching for possible innovations known to us from other industries. Whole sectors allow their innovation processes to be guided by advisors and directors, beginning with a targeted search for new inventions and ending with the completed product, building on theories such as TRIZ (Theory of Inventive Problem Solving, conceived by Genrich Altschuller in 1946) or TOC (Theory of Constraints, conceived by E. Goldratt in 1986) and orienting their development strategy accordingly [41].

If we acknowledge this fact, and respond by trying to liberate our innovation development processes from an individual or chance-driven development pattern, it is important to recognize the determining parameters of these processes. If this can be achieved, then, for instance, solutions that are already known to us from one area of construction can be applied to another. Alternatively, we could systematically examine technologies from other branches of the sciences to assess whether they have any value for construction and the

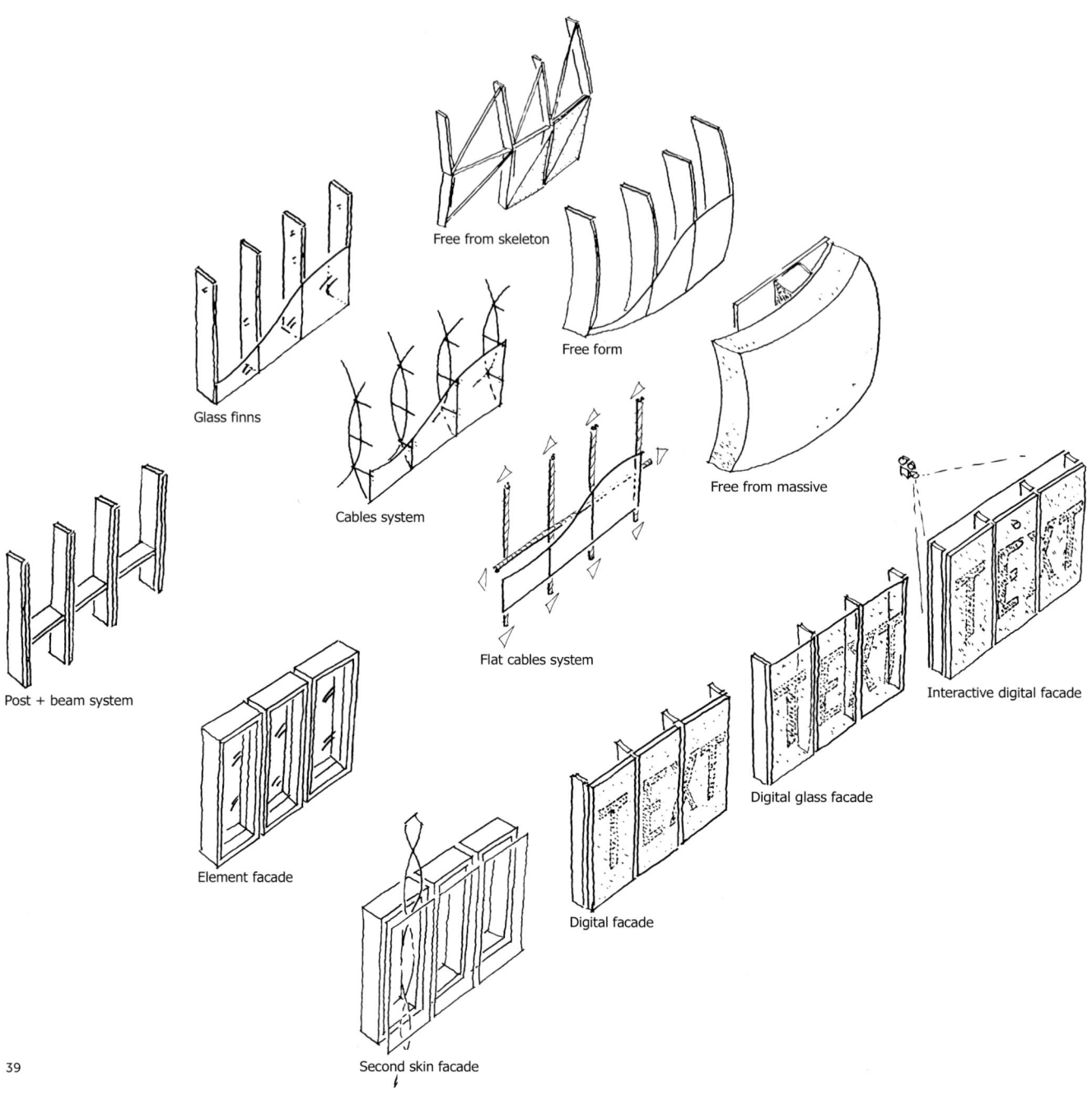

Free from skeleton

Free form

Free from massive

Glass finns

Cables system

Flat cables system

Post + beam system

Interactive digital facade

Digital glass facade

Digital facade

Element facade

Second skin facade

39

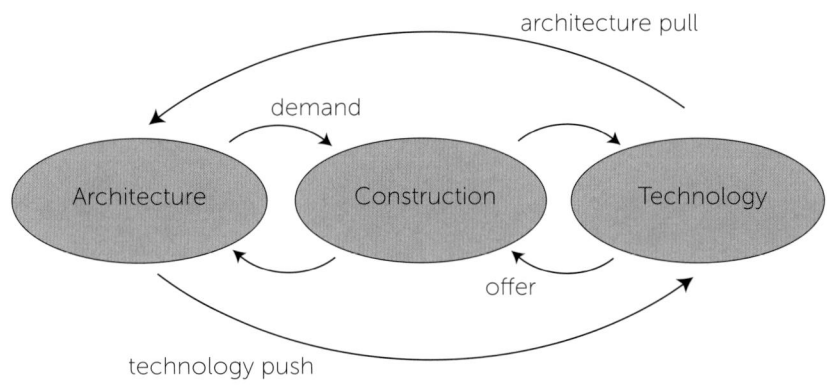

architecture pull

demand

Architecture   Construction   Technology

offer

technology push

40

40 Pull-push mechanism
adapted for Tillmann Klein /
TU Delft building envelope

potential benefits of adopting them, and doing so where appropriate. If neither approach achieves the desired goal, then it will be necessary to develop alternative solution scenarios, possibly involving developing a new technology.

The *facade road map* concept presented here as a method follows this approach. In addition to identifying development patterns and tracing long-term development progressions, it endeavors to generate new possibilities, to identify new connections and missing building blocks and possible future scenarios for development. Admittedly this approach can offer no answers to the question of which of the developments that promise to deliver potential innovations are worth pursuing and which are interesting only in a purely academic sense, with no economic or social significance: the difficulty lies partly in the risks of evaluating a social consensus that constantly shifts its focus, and partly in the fact that economic processes depend only to a limited extent on technological development and are also subject to significant (politically motivated) reversals. At present, for instance, we find ourselves in an era in which special attention is given to energy issues, but we can already see the conservation of water resources emerging as the next major topic, without as yet being able to assess fully all aspects of water conservation's impact on construction.

As there is no possibility of solving this problem in a long-term and universally applicable way, the road map described here must be regarded as an instrument for dynamic development steerage. It enables an appraisal of the subject matter but will remain subject to change due to changes of direction and changing perspectives on trends.

Developing
Ideas

Curved Planes

Christoph Schindler
Jan Bieniek

Vision

The need to produce curved forms from level materials has presented many architects, designers, and engineers with a challenge – particularly in the twentieth century. The addition of individual digital production to industrial serial production at the turn of the millennium made the manufacture of curved forms – without the need for molds – an enticing prospect.

Methods

The ZipShape method is based on a simple geometrical idea. A molded body consists of two panels toothed in such a way that they will fit together only at the desired curvature. The curvature is determined by the difference in the angles on the tooth sides. After joining, there are no cavities or openings in the molding body volume – making the process different from methods that involve regular slits (such as Glunz's Topan MDF Form [42], Daniel Michalik's Cortiça chaise [43] or Christian Kuhn's and Serge Lunin's Dukta [44]), and from concepts that allow sheet metals to be bent to conform to a predetermined geometry (such as Florian Tschacher's La Chaise [45] or ROK's Flat2Form [46]).

With its repeatable but individual details, ZipShape is tailor-made for generative modeling. A parametric model can be used to derive the logical detailing from any given output curve. All of the details are parametrically recorded and can therefore be adapted at any time.

1

2

1 A ZipShape molded body consists of two panels toothed in such a way that they will fit together only at the desired curvature. The ZipChaise is constructed from solid laminated oak with a thickness of 20mm. Schreinerei Bach Heiden with Schilliger Holz AG, Küssnacht am Rigi, July 2007

2 The Ziprocker, developed with R. Aimer, K. von Felde, O. Illner, S. Rehders, T. Schütt and H. Wolf, is a projecting rocking chair with an overall material thickness of 30mm, composed from a spruce middle layer between two layers of walnut veneer. This shape was derived from that of a car seat. Fachschule für Holztechnik, Hamburg, January 2009.

At the heart of the standard production strategy for ZipShape panels is either a five-axis lathe (a saw blade for the teeth edges, a flat nose end mill for the tooth base), or a three-axis lathe with parallel finishing perpendicular to the direction of the teeth. In spite of the beauty of the constructive logic behind ZipShapes, both methods are time-intensive. As the curvature is defined by the geometry of the teeth, the mold normally used during the drying of the glue can be replaced by a vacuum sack, which acts as a flexible mold.

Possible materials were considered, and wood was chosen. The good machinability of timber also made it highly suitable for cutting with a lathe – the planned method of construction. A number of toothed MDF, plywood, and solid laminated wood panels were successfully curved to a radius of 5–20 times the thickness of the material (although the tighter of these radii had a pronounced tendency to break). This, however, is impressive when one considers that the maximum radius that can generally be achieved in the cold bending of wood is 50 times the material's thickness [47], [48].

The Ziprocker, created in a course at the Fachschule für Holztechnik Hamburg (Hamburg school of timber technology), is a particularly impressive prototype. Two covering layers of deciduous wood veneer (cherry or walnut) and a coniferous wood middle layer (spruce) were laminated; the additional rigidity allowed a radius of five times the material's thickness while safeguarding the rocking chair's load-bearing ability. This resulted in widespread approbation and a series of awards [49], but further examination showed that the quality of the end product was still unsatisfactory: the panels only bent between the teeth, giving the

3

4

3 Recoflex is a compound material composed of wood, cork and latex particles. It is fairly elastic, but it becomes rigid as soon as veneer is applied. ETH RAPLAB, Zurich, July 2010

4 The ZipLiege chaise is constructed from an 18mm Recoflex middle layer with glued ash veneer. Its shape is derived from human proportions. It was sawn in five sections at the Schreinerei Schnidrig in Visp and vacuum-laminated at the BFH–AHB in Biel. Designers' Saturday 2010, Langenthal, November 2010

surfaces a polygonal appearance. The tight radii placed too much stress on the wood fibers on the surfaces, and the veneer tended to develop hairline cracks on the outside of the curves and to warp on the inside of the curve. Cold bending the panels also required the physical efforts of three people.

Innovation

The realization that the same construction principle could have different outcomes for different materials caused the universal status of ZipShapes to be revised, and the selection of the right materials to be incorporated into the process as a necessary step.

As a consequence, it became clear that the toothed cross-section of a ZipShape panel must consist of two separate areas – the teeth and the thin layer that holds them together. In order to define the geometrical structure, the teeth had to be elastic yet pressure-resistant, and the connecting layers had to withstand tension while remaining flexible.

For the middle layer, a product known as Recoflex was used: a compound material composed of wood, cork, and latex particles. This material is fairly elastic, but it becomes rigid as soon as veneer is laminated onto it.

This combination of a wood-cork-latex compound material with facing veneer was tested intensively for its suitability for the production of two large ZipLiege

5

5 The CNC hot wire cutter provided by Stepfour GmbH can be used to prepare any standard surface. Detmold School of Architecture and Interior Design in association with the University of Florida, May 2011

chaises. Both objects were given a ZipShape Recoflex middle layer with ash veneer on both sides. This allowed the radius to be reduced to a material thickness to radius proportion of 1/3 (a minimum radius of 75mm for a material thickness of 24mm). The elasticity of the wood/cork/latex middle layer makes a clear difference to the user, helping to make the object more comfortable. This is surprising to the user, as the facing veneer provides no clue to this aspect of the piece's character.

The ZipLiege case study investigated a production speed of 1.1m per hour for a material thickness of 0.6m (equal to 0.7m²/h), using a five-axis lathe — insufficient for an economically viable working process.

A workshop held at the Detmold School of Architecture and Interior Design in May 2011 provided the opportunity to find a production concept that did not require the lathe. Extruded hard polystyrene foam (XPS) was generally used for the middle layer, with the teeth cut into it by means of a large CNC hot wire cutter. A hot wire cutter can cut the whole of the ZipShape profile in a single working phase without the need to change tools, cutting production time to 4.4m per hour — four times faster than the five-axis lathe. Polystyrene is quick and easy to prepare, as well as being lightweight and inexpensive. However, it cannot be compared to wood or wood-derived products in terms of surface haptic properties, stability, and sustainability.

The CNC hot wire cutter is capable of producing standardized surfaces, and is therefore particularly of interest in the case of undulating shapes, for which the

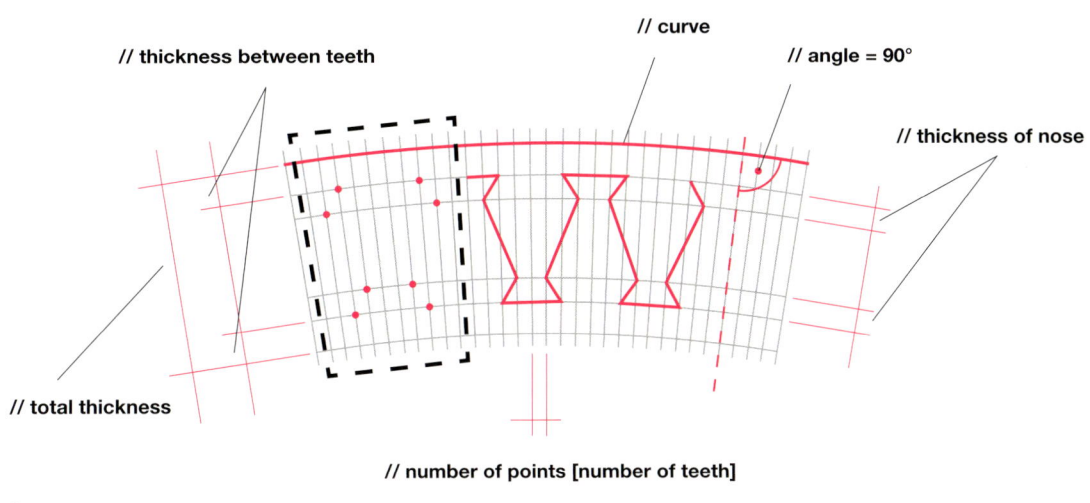

// thickness between teeth

// curve

// angle = 90°

// thickness of nose

// total thickness

// number of points [number of teeth]

6

6 Programming variants 1, grid- and point-oriented: *thickness of nose* describes the thickness of the "barbs", *total thickness* describes the total thickness of the assembled product, *number of points* defines the grade of the grid (and therefore the number of points), *thickness between teeth* affects the breadth of the individual tines

teeth sides are not level and can therefore not be sawn. In order to make the XPS molding bodies sufficiently tension-resistant, veneer was once again applied on both sides to serve as facing. A wide field of experimentation had now been opened up with regard to joins that cannot be produced through sawing. In particular, the focus was on snap-lock connections, which allowed the two panels to be interlocked without needing to be additionally secured. The Klick-Zip procedure has potential in a number of different respects:

> it avoids the need for the costly and time-intensive vacuum sack gluing process;
> the joining process can be relocated to the application site, reducing transport volumes and significantly simplifying protection during transport;
> temporary connections are a possibility; these would allow a wide variety of requirements, situations, and needs to be responded to quickly and flexibly.

On the other hand, this procedure imposes increased requirements on the medium: it must be stable in order to ensure that the connections do not separate (especially in the case of tight radii, for which significant forces can occur). At the same time, it must be flexible.

No specific results had previously been obtained for models on a 1:1 scale. An inner angle measurement of between 130° and 160° enables the teeth to fit smoothly together while ensuring support.

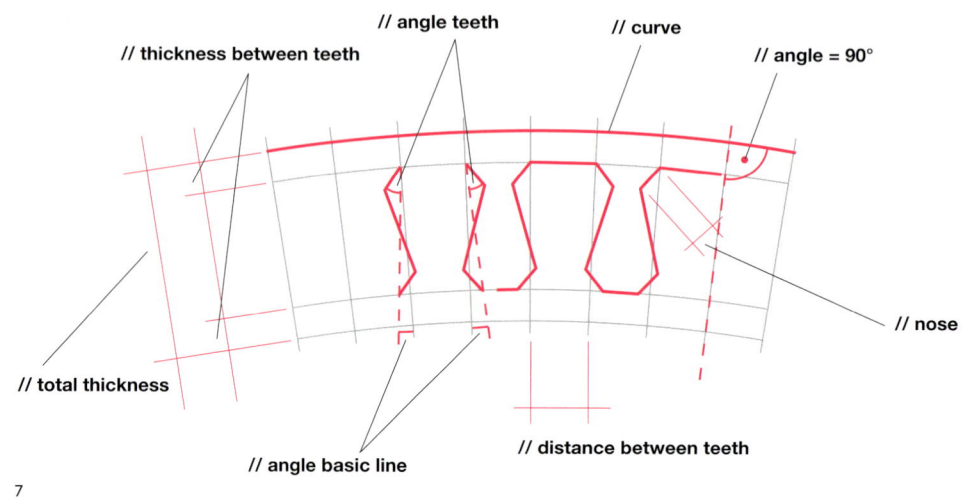

// thickness between teeth
// angle teeth
// curve
// angle = 90°
// nose
// total thickness
// angle basic line
// distance between teeth

7

7 Programming variant 2, line-oriented: *nose* describes the thickness of the "barbs", *total thickness* describes the total thickness of the assembled product, *number of points* defines the grade of the grid (and therefore the number of points), *thickness between teeth* affects the breadth of the individual tines, *angle basic line* defines the angle of orientation, *angle teeth*, in turn, describes the angle of spread for this particular direction

The conclusion to a paper published in 2008 proposed the investigation of general preparation of standardized surfaces, reduction of the radius, and experiments with materials other than wood and wood-derived materials [50]. All three points have been investigated. No other known cold-bending process permits a comparable radius-to-material-thickness ratio. In the course of working toward these goals, the existing results were taken into account and the following conclusions were reached:

From geometry to experience – ZipShape having initially been conceived as an abstract geometrical model, an awareness subsequently developed of the need to take account of production conditions and of how to create designs actively, incorporating knowledge of material properties – with form, material, and production technique treated as an indivisible system. One particularly surprising finding was that the impact of each of the various material and production factors could not be predicted with absolute precision. Once materials and production techniques have been taken into account, the coherent geometrical model must be abandoned.

From the university to the market, or: the path is the goal – the project, which, thus far, has consisted of four invitation-only workshops and a number of lectures, can currently be considered an academic success, and has been recognized by a series of awards. The clear way in which it combines material and information processing appears to epitomize the modern attitude to architecture and to product design.

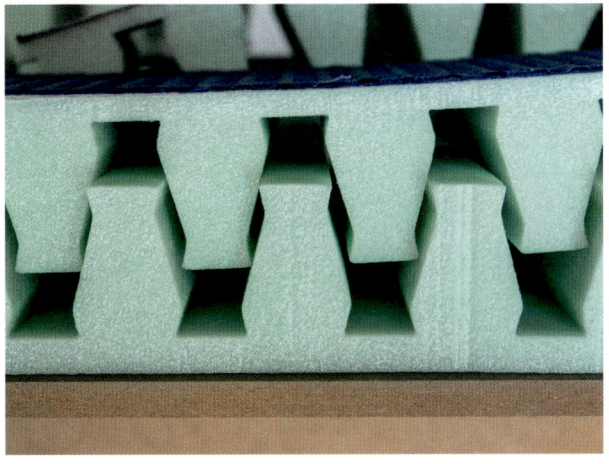

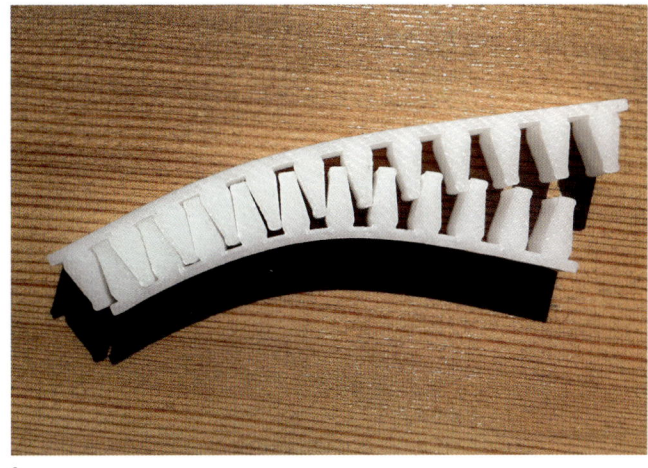

8

9

8 KlickZip hot wire-cut snap lock
system by J. Bieniek, F. Nienhaus,
L. A. Pinkcombe and A. Wood,
Detmold School of Architecture
and Interior Design in association
with the University of Florida,
May 2011

9 KlickZip pattern in thermo-
plastic ABS from the 3D printer,
Detmold School of Architecture
and Interior Design in association
with the University of Florida,
May 2011

Introducing ZipShapes to the market, however, has proved to be more complex than expected. The perfect combination of materials has not yet been found. One has the impression that this process is not a candidate for replacing existing technologies in existing areas of application. Where ZipShapes do possess potential is in the search for novel applications based on specific properties.

Acknowledgments

schindlersalmerón is a private furniture manufacturer with a limited research operation. Without the opportunity to hold workshops at a series of academic institutions, the project would not have been possible. We are grateful to all those who helped in this. Our particular thanks goes to Marco Hemmerling of the Detmold School of Architecture and Interior Design for providing access to the Detmold Workshop and the CNC hot wire cutter, and to Stepfour GmbH.

The Rediscovery of Known Materials

Christian Grabitz
Christina Kröger

Vision

The Arbeitsgemeinschaft Blechprofilroste (ABR) or "Sheet metal grids working group" brings together leading German and European manufacturers, and is responsible for producing the RAL-GZ 639 quality assurance system. The aim of their collaboration with students of the International Facade Design and Construction (IFDC) master's degree program at the Detmold School of Architecture and Interior Design was to develop new ideas for the individualized application of standardized industrial products in building envelopes. The companies are acting in the light of an increasingly significant trend toward internationalization in the market, which presents new challenges to those concerned with distribution, technology development, and production. The combination of teaching and practice in this workshop was pioneering in that it brought together a total of twenty-four master's students from fourteen nations (including Spain, Hungary, Thailand, Bangladesh, India, Jordan, and Iran) in order to engage with this issue. The students also brought to the table their own qualifications and preparatory training: their studies in architecture, architectural engineering, metal construction technology, construction engineering, and design.

Sheet metal profile grids have previously been used primarily as nonslip floors and floor-covering materials in industrial, commercial, and vehicle construction, and for walkways, platforms, and stairs. Their use in offices and administrative buildings or in special buildings is fairly rare, and even rarer in facades. Examples, however, show that these products possess considerable potential in design and construction terms — potential that has hitherto largely remained unexploited. Advantages of sheet metal profile grids include their combination of low materi-

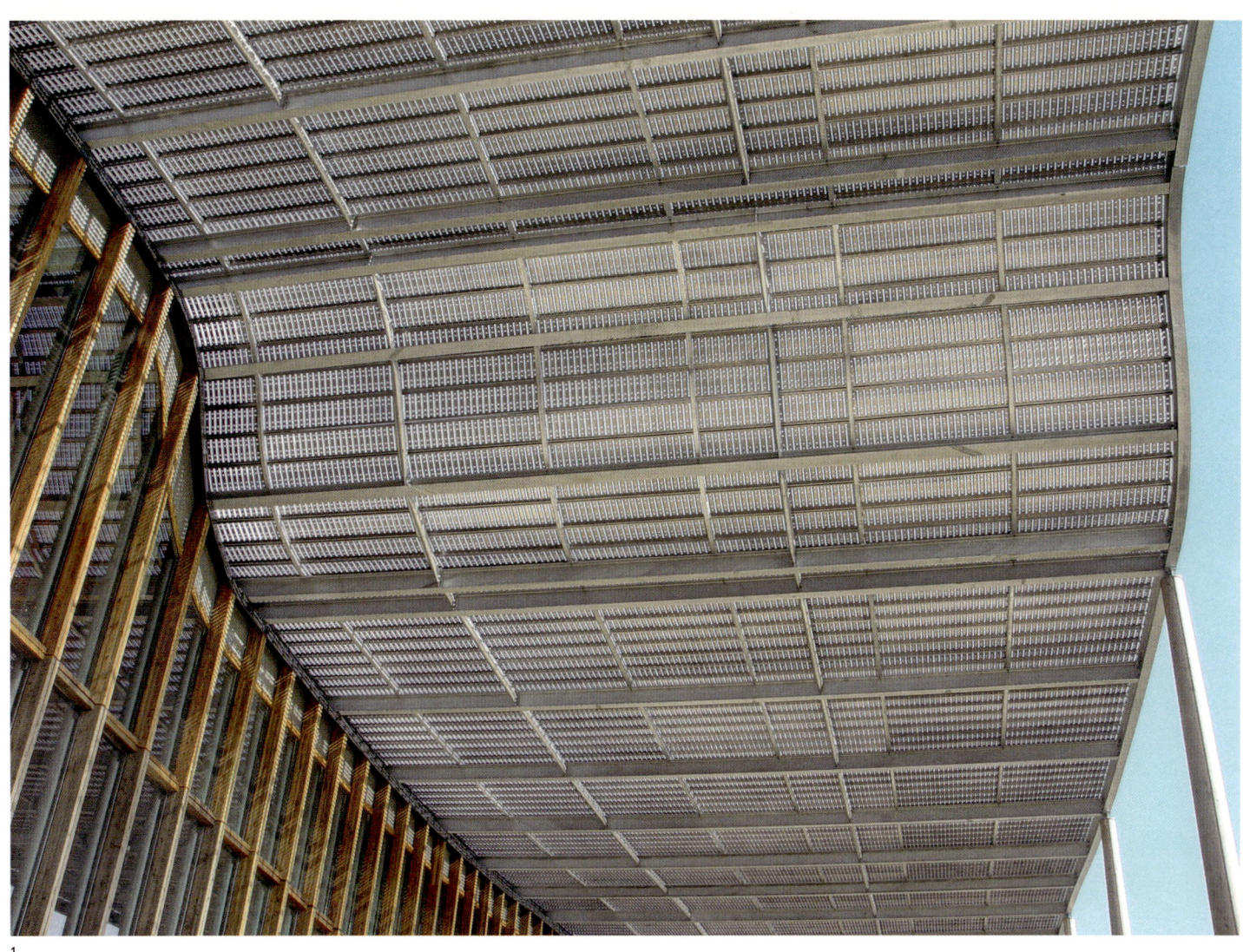

1

7 Danone laboratories, Palaiseau.
Architect: Architecture Studio,
Paris. Construction variants:
SIMO SIRO/P 300 × 50 × 2 grid
in rough aluminum, SIMO Blech-
verarbeitung GmbH

2

3

4

5

6

7

2 "The Human Network,"
Utrecht. Architect: Atelier Dutch
Almere and Centrum Architecten.
Product: Staco Holding B.V.

3 Mooring jetty in Bregenz.
Architect: Nägele Waibel ZT
GmbH. Product: Lichtgitter
GmbH

4 Messeparkhaus Frankfurt
(multistory parking garage for
trade convention use). Architect:
Eisenman. Product: Lichtgitter
GmbH

5 CHU Hospital, Dijon. Architect: Groupe 6, Paris. Product:
SIMO Blechverarbeitung GmbH

6 Brainstorming and ideation
process

7 Participants of the workshop
at the Detmolder Schule für
Architektur und Innenarchitektur
in collaboration with ABR

8　　　　　　　　　　　　　9

8, 9 Extension to Museum of Military History, Dresden. Architect: Daniel Libeskind. Product: Graepel-STUV GmbH

als use and high load-bearing capacity – enabled by the C-profile cross section, which permits span lengths of up to nine meters. Additionally, sheet metal profile grids manufactured from galvanized steel or precious metals are maintenance-free products with a long useful life, which can be temporarily or permanently secured to any backing so that surface form and design can be varied.

Possible facade-related applications include shading elements, access routes, and connective passageways, as well as wall cladding and panels – both for new buildings and for modernizing existing buildings.

Both sides profited from the workshop collaboration. The primary goal was to find and to visualize new ideas and applications for further product development. The method, however, can also be used to facilitate quicker implementation of innovative solutions and to help both the companies and the students to acquire knowledge to equip themselves for the future. The bringing together of technicians, distributors, planners, and students facilitated interdisciplinary and comprehensive perspectives. The companies involved benefited from new insights into a variety of markets and user groups, and the students benefited from direct contact with the companies. The work they produced also had strong links to industry practice.

Methods

In order to do justice to existing and future building envelopes requirements, the project was linked to a specific IFDC master's degree semester project: an

 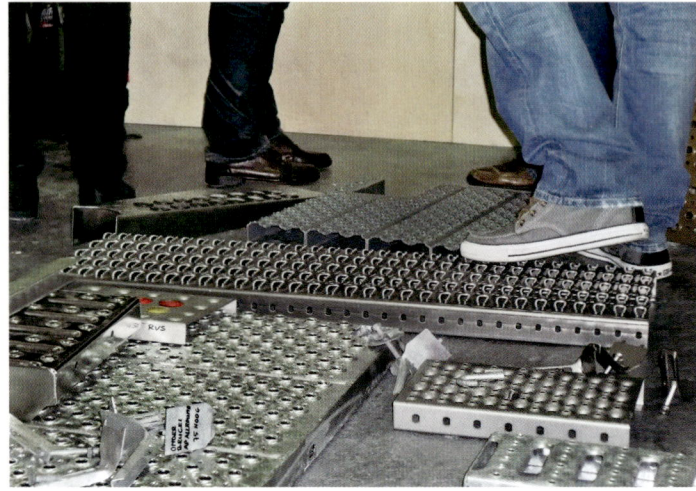

10   11

10, 11 Sheet profile grids:
product variants

energy optimization and facade restoration plan for an office building dating from the 1980s. In addition, the state of technological development in available sheet metal profile grids was a significant predetermining factor for further development of the new products. Representatives of the four companies included in the working group – Graepel-STUV GmbH, Lichtgitter GmbH, SIMO Blechverarbeitung GmbH, and Staco Holding B.V. – therefore provided an introduction to the manufacture, processing, and previous applications of sheet metal profile grid products.

A preliminary brainstorming session was held in order to come up with ideas. During the initial creative process, fundamental design principles, needs, and criteria were defined (with an emphasis on specific markets or target groups), and early drafts of the restoration concepts identified specific needs in design and product development. The students separated into eight work groups and came up with a variety of ideas and potential applications.

Results

The students taking part in the workshop presented a wide variety of solutions, which then had to be refined in the subsequent development stage, with a view to a possible constructive and technology-related production implementation. These involved combining sheet metal profile grids with LED backlighting or with greening elements, and with fixed or mobile shading elements. Taken together, these ideas allowed particular creative approaches to be identified as being particularly worth pursuing:

12   13

12, 13 Idea: a specimen facade composed of sections; Panos Sakkas, TU Delft, Daniel Palma Ramirez and Surachat Gumngen, Hochschule OWL

> applying suitable design to existing products (ornamenting);
> the reversal of existing design principles ("patchwork");
> new ways of combining known materials and functions (LED lighting, glass-metal combination, greening);
> scaling up conventional product dimensions (the development of facade "zones");
> perforation geometries as determiners of function (sun protection);
> the visualization of a double skin at night (lit supports).

Starting with the terms *modular* and *lawn*, one group visualized an approach that responded to the less-than-optimal situations associated with the existing building through an economical amalgamation of functions. Their self-imposed goal was to create compact courtyard areas adjoining the building, to enable connections between forward and recessed sections of the construction. This compact geometry makes sense in energy terms, and also creates new spaces to a high standard for users. Once other important criteria for an up-to-date building envelope had been taken into account, this design created a possible application for sheet metal profile grids, which have the advantage of being cost-effective and simple to install and to remove, and also allow the microclimate of the modified areas of the complex to be improved by means of planting.

The results show that members of the ABR group and the students at the three locations taking part – Detmold, Delft and Lucerne – profited considerably from the exchange. The international and interdisciplinary philosophy also generated a particular kind of added value in that the wide variety of approaches made a significant contribution to the development of creative ideas.

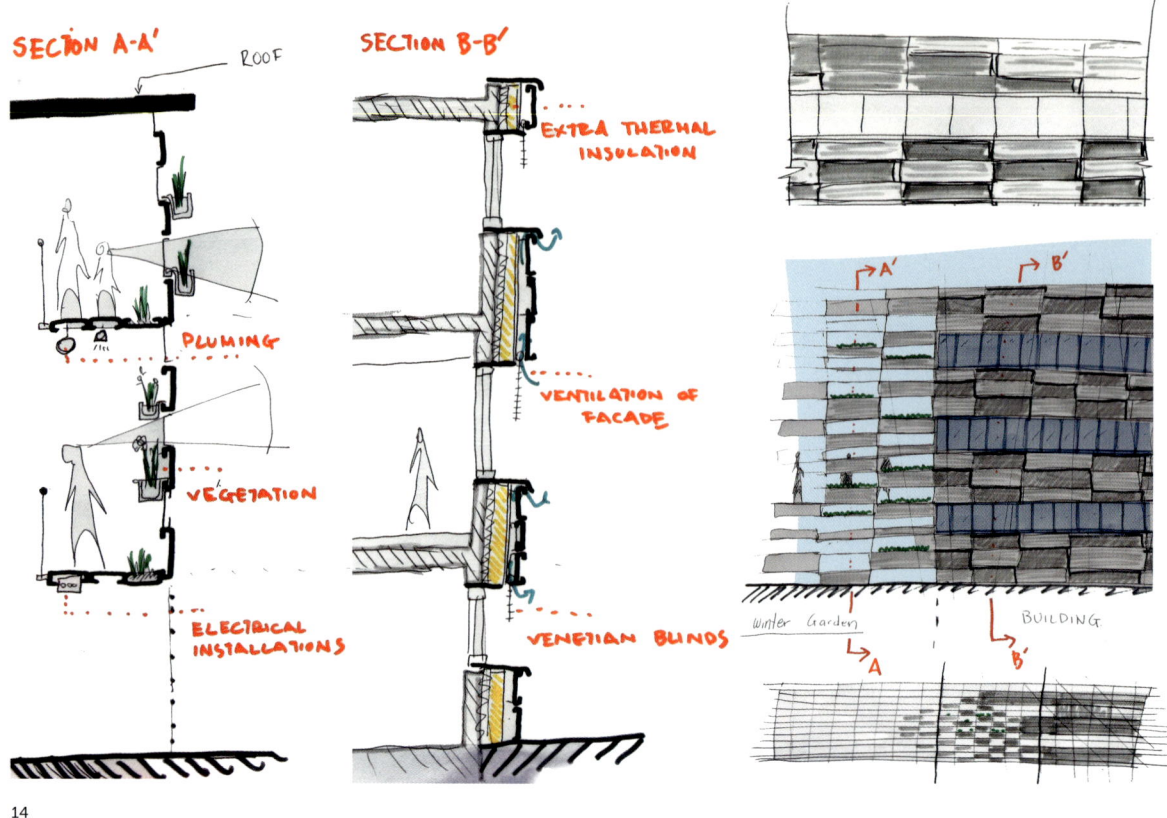

SECTION A-A'   ROOF

SECTION B-B'

EXTRA THERMAL INSULATION

PLUMING

VENTILATION OF FACADE

VEGETATION

VENETIAN BLINDS

ELECTRICAL INSTALLATIONS

A'   B'

Winter Garden   BUILDING

A   B'

14

14 A combined glass and metal facade

Innovation

During the workshop stage itself, samples and presentation objects were constructed in order to carry out tests and to improve visualization. This permanent intercommunication of two- and three-dimensional representations was material to steering the further development and revision of ideas, allowing novel visual, haptic, and acoustic effects to be demonstrated in a credible manner – a major factor in connecting with new target groups and markets. Like other aspects of the project, optimizing the combination of know-how, technology, and design is a stage-by-stage development process.

Following the workshop, the students assessed and categorized the degree of innovation contained in the essentials of their ideas and the timeframe that would be required to implement them. This process provides the basis for further discussions with the companies, who will assess the feasibility of specific implementations of individual proposals after making an evaluation of their own.

The workshop has in any case demonstrated that the future of sheet metal profile grids does not lie solely in horizontal applications (such as floor coverings), and that vertical situations such as facade design also offer the possibility for a number of different applications. The members of the Arbeitsgemeinschaft Blechprofilroste sheet metal profile grid work group have already demonstrated that their products can be used in facade design. The students have provided the impetus for the next stage – the development of function-specific facades using sheet metal grid profiles.

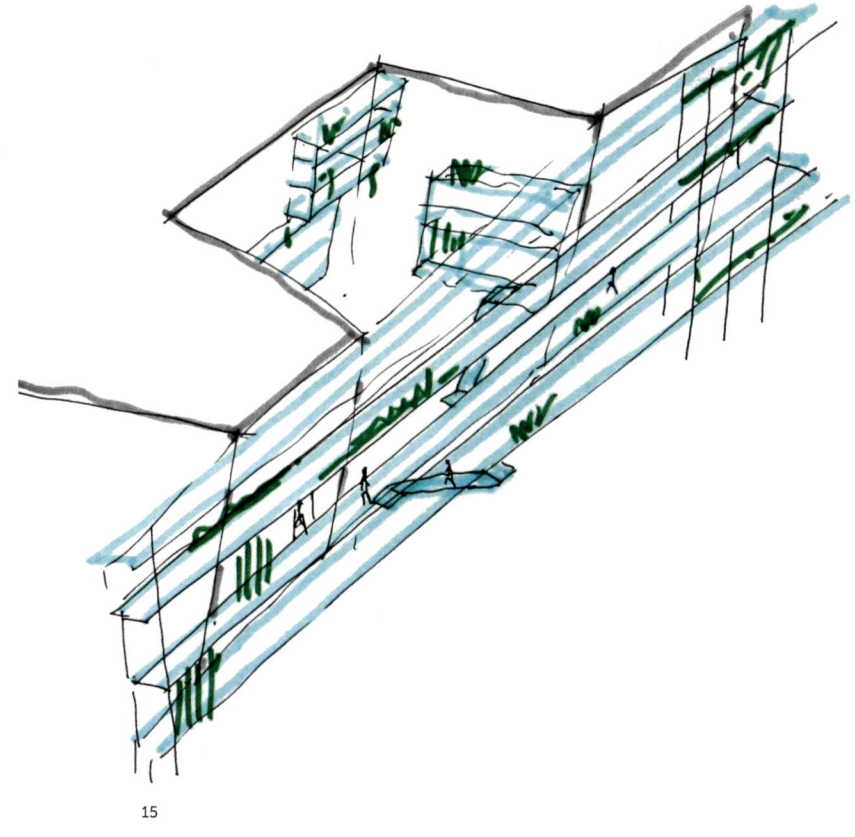

15

16

17

18

15 The courtyard element is
defined by a superimposed sheet
metal grid facade.

16–18 Idea: LED backlighting;
Alejandro Cabello Carretero,
Hochschule OWL, Wang Yajie,
TU Delft, Paul Jurisic, Lucerne
University of Applied Arts and
Sciences

Redefining
Boundaries

Total Building Envelope

Winfried Heusler
Steve Lo

Vision

In the new millennium, we have been living through a third wave of globalization, which is characterized by a state of permanent technological change, with personal devices, the Internet, and an extremely fast and economically viable fibre optics network at its heart. This state of permanent technological change goes hand in hand with new expectations from users and changes in what is required from the built environment. The greatest challenge that this third wave of globalization has brought with it is that of implementing an urban or building plan that is sustainable in all its aspects – ecologically, economically, and socioculturally – throughout the lifetime of the planning object:

> From the ecological perspective, what is required is a design that makes sparing use of resources.
> From the economic perspective, cost-effective solutions – optimization of initial outlay and life cycle costs – are the long-term goal.
> From the sociocultural perspective, the form and aesthetic of the building – including issues of cultural preservation – are key. These issues are closely linked with the comfort of users who inhabit and function within the building and with healthy home and workplace conditions.

Concepts and products that ensure energy efficiency and material efficiency and structures and buildings with highly efficient planning, construction, and operation processes are required. Development work currently focuses on communication between construction components and building automation

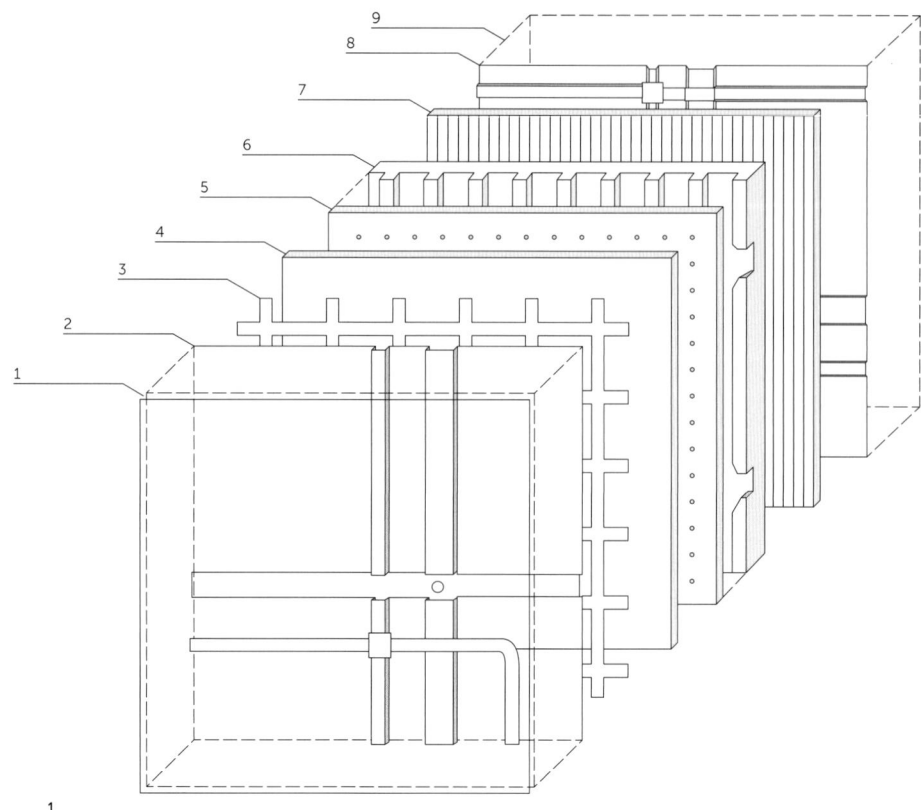

1 Thermal sheet radiator / selective absorber
2 Silica weather skin and deposition substrate
3 Electro-reflective deposition
4 Sensor and control logic layer, external
5 Photoelectric grid
6 Micro-pore gas-flow layer
7 Electro-reflective deposition
8 Sensor and control logic layer, internal

1

**1 Layer structure schematic
for polyvalent wall**

and their responsiveness to users. The facade is a particularly important part of the implementation of a total building design – because its visibility and impact makes it a crucial part of the building's identity, and because it exerts such a major influence on energy efficiency, material efficiency, process efficiency and cost efficiency.

Method

The challenge is to develop a facade engineering design process by empowering all the disciplines and sectors involved to resolve specific building envelope issues. Such practices are employed mostly in large companies working on large-scale multinational projects. Their size allows specialist facade engineering and building services contractors to be engaged early in the design process. Nevertheless, it is mostly in smaller and less prestigious projects that difficulties in technical understanding and communication are encountered during the design process, occasioned by the presence of multiple professionals with conflicting discipline-related interests. Without the in-house expertise of large design practices, the standard facade design process in an SME means the architect and the specialist facade envelope contractor are involved in numerous iterative decision-making loops. Insufficient technical knowledge and guidance within these – often small – architectural and engineering practices, which must rely on feedback from the envelope contractor to resolve issues at every stage of the design and specification process, create looped discussions of every facade component. Additional consultation loops arise between the fa-

Sustainability aspects for building envelopes

lifecycle	ecologic	economic	sociocultural
raw materials / semi-finished			
production / processing			
manufacturing / mounting			
use / maintenance			
refurbishment			
demolishing/ demounting			
recycling			

2

2 Life cycle analysis as the key to a sustainable building plan (beam length is shown to illustrate the significance of the different issues)

cade envelope contractor and the facade component supplier. Conflicting feedback from the client, the architect, the facade systems specialist, and the many disciplines involved in the design process makes it difficult to arrive at a consensus. This lack of full understanding inhibits the productive collaboration and synergy between all parties required for a holistic building design process. The loop that exists for each and every component is a complex process. The results of decisions in each loop also have an impact on many of the other facade component decision-making loops. Ultimately, the designer resides a long way from the supplier. This fragmented approach and lack of embedded technical and design expertise hinders meaningful long-term synergies, making optimal design solutions difficult to incorporate at the later stages of the design [51].

It was in 1981 that the adaptable polyvalent wall building shell system was first introduced to the discussion (by British architect Mike Davies). Its extremely thin functional layers regulate the flow of energy between the indoor and outdoor environment, and adapt themselves to changing climate conditions without the need for intervention. This marked the beginning of a phase where researchers and developers worked with materials and components that respond to external conditions, automatically regulating light and heat permeability, air exchange and sound transmission to ensure optimum energy and materials efficiency. Facade engineering is a multidisciplinary industry involving architects, engineers, specialist contractors, and consultants. This discipline is key to ensuring holistic building design – to resolving aesthetic, environmental, and structural issues by developing a solution that ensures a sustainable enclosure for a habitable space.

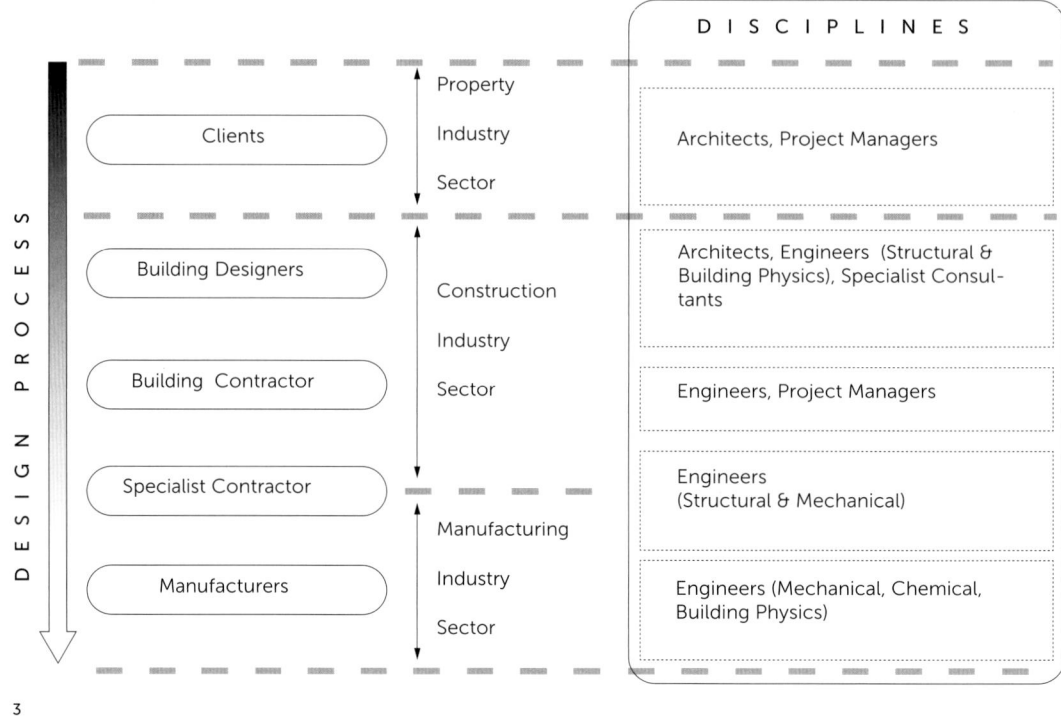

DISCIPLINES

Clients	Architects, Project Managers
Building Designers	Architects, Engineers (Structural & Building Physics), Specialist Consultants
Building Contractor	Engineers, Project Managers
Specialist Contractor	Engineers (Structural & Mechanical)
Manufacturers	Engineers (Mechanical, Chemical, Building Physics)

Property Industry Sector

Construction Industry Sector

Manufacturing Industry Sector

DESIGN PROCESS

3

3 Facade engineering sectors and disciplines involved in the design process

It requires a detailed knowledge of design, materials, fabrication, and installation. These disciplines encompass many sectors, which operate more and more at an international level.

An increase in requests for research in this area – especially from SMEs involved in the sector, such as small architectural practices, engineering consultants, and specialist facade contractors – reveals industry-driven demand for more unified design processes and guidance. There is a clear need to unify the disparate knowledge, education, and research at this level so that an integrated and fully supported facade engineering design process may emerge. This will enable science and industry to strive toward a common education and research framework for a more integrated building envelope design process. It also allows for novel and bespoke designs to be achieved through transparent and embedded levels of technical communication and for greater understanding between the design and construction teams. The proposed joint research initiative and Ph.D. project ToBE (Total Building Envelope) aims to contribute to the challenges of a holistic building design by enhancing knowledge and knowledge transfer in facade engineering.

Results

Reconciling all the disparate design approaches involves bringing all the disciplines concerned with building envelope design together to pool and exchange their substantial individual knowledge within a single framework of

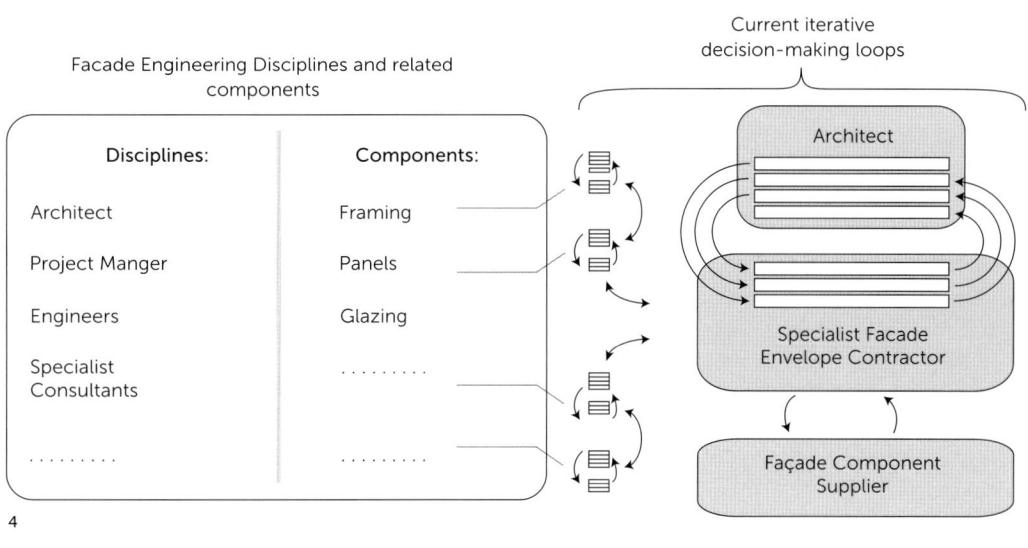

Facade Engineering Disciplines and related components

Current iterative decision-making loops

4

4 The complexity of decision making iterations between the various actors in the design team

experts, academics, and clients. This framework – the European Facade Network (EFN) – was founded in 2009 in Brussels, in an initiative originating from European universities that have established facade-related teaching programs (University of Bath, TU Delft, the University of the Basque Country, Hochschule Ostewestfalen-Lippe, and the Hochschule Luzern). The network is accomplished by the transfer of engineers and practitioners from commercial facade engineering sectors into a neutral academic environment with an overarching multidisciplinary direction. The framework involves identifying and discussing the gaps that exist in the concept, the appropriate technical guidance, and design tools, with the development and application of a common design language at every stage of the design process.

The resultant synergies will allow the process-led technical guidance and design tools required for an integrated environmental facade engineering and design to emerge. The framework aims to bridge the knowledge and communication gap between architects and designers, engineers, and building specialists, and the facade engineering industry by empowering the educational system at master's and Ph.D. level by promoting broader knowledge. The repository of knowledge thus produced will promote interdisciplinary cooperation between specialists with backgrounds in different disciplines and give them the confidence to engage in a more design-rich dialogue that uses a common design language, ensuring less ambiguity and confusion. This turning-inward is an essential precondition for the development of an appropriate and optimal building envelope as an integral part of a holistic building design.

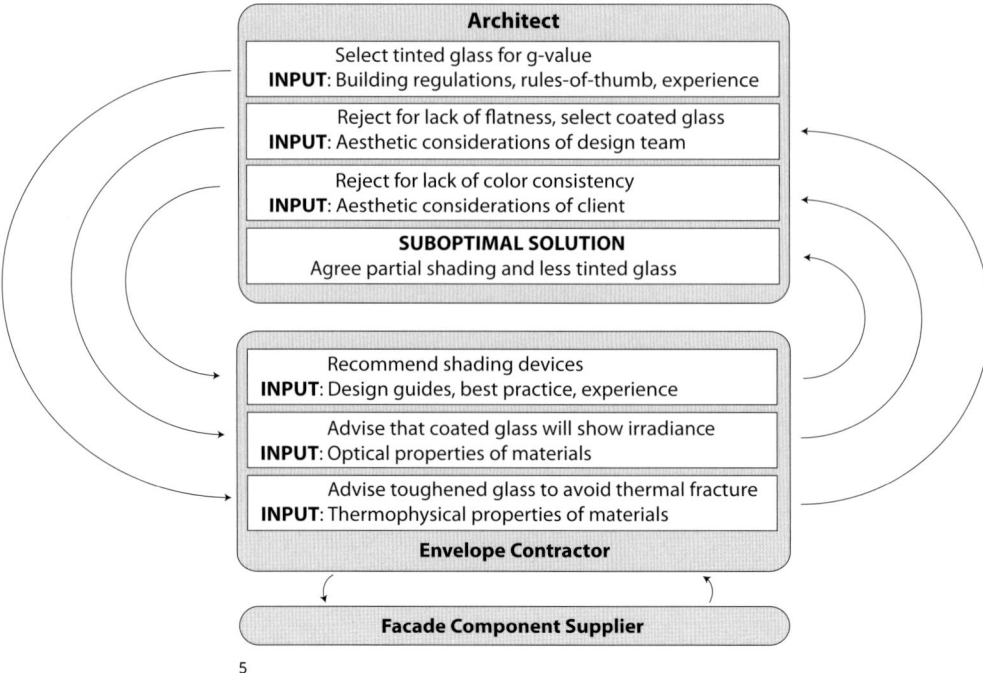

Architect

| Select tinted glass for g-value |
| **INPUT:** Building regulations, rules-of-thumb, experience |

| Reject for lack of flatness, select coated glass |
| **INPUT:** Aesthetic considerations of design team |

| Reject for lack of color consistency |
| **INPUT:** Aesthetic considerations of client |

| **SUBOPTIMAL SOLUTION** |
| Agree partial shading and less tinted glass |

| Recommend shading devices |
| **INPUT:** Design guides, best practice, experience |

| Advise that coated glass will show irradiance |
| **INPUT:** Optical properties of materials |

| Advise toughened glass to avoid thermal fracture |
| **INPUT:** Thermophysical properties of materials |

Envelope Contractor

Facade Component Supplier

5

5 The feedback loops between the architect, the specialist facade envelope contractor, and the facade component supplier

Efficiency or sufficiency strategy

The problem-solving approaches that have been introduced into the wider discussion to promote a unified building design adopt either an efficiency strategy or a sufficiency strategy [52]. The efficiency strategy begins with an analysis of the planning, construction, and operation of the building, aiming to minimize wastage of energy, materials, money, and time – a product-centered design approach. The sufficiency strategy, on the other hand, begins with an analysis of the behavior of individuals, with the aim of reducing the consumption of resources for a sustainable future – a human-centered design approach. Fields in which these could make a contribution include:

> energy efficiency through optimization of user comfort, solar protection, and daylighting, addition of buffer zones and modification of the building's thermal and physical boundaries, automatic and adaptive building automation, integration and optimization of renewable energy technologies;
> material and process efficiency through minimization of materials used for building and increased durability and recycling potential of the components, using the "garbage" of maintenance and modernization measures as an archive of resources, and a more flexible production that could be better adapted to specific needs;
> eco-sufficiency through a reduction of consumption to save natural resources, goods, and materials by changing the user's and society's way of living, and empowering the users to embed more intuitive energy-efficient building operations.

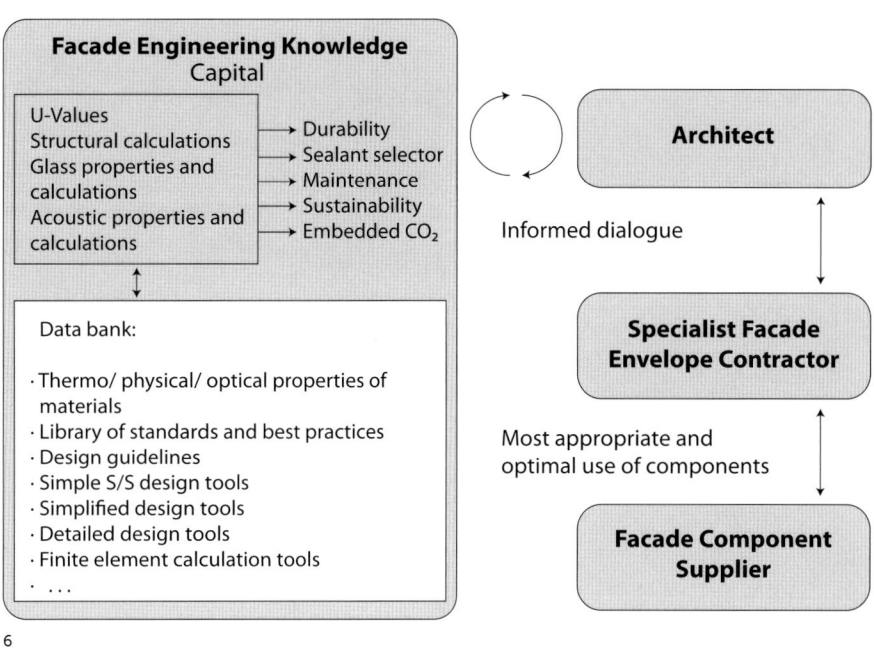

6

6 Interface between the facade engineering knowledge capital design portal and the architect

All these topics will be investigated within the planned Ph.D. program ToBE (Total Building Envelope) of the European Facade Network:

> Design & process: Design strategies for new and existing lifetime low-carbon building envelopes.
> An integrated system-level, low-carbon knowledge-driven design process for new building envelopes
> Low-carbon refurbishment of existing building envelopes

Interfaces in the planning process

Structures: Maximizing structural efficiency of the building envelope and its components
> Low-carbon structurally efficient facade elements
> Structural bonded glass profiles with composite action

Materials: Embedding systems-based life-time carbon assessment into sustainable procurement to reduce building envelope carbon emissions
> Design for achievable economic lifetime durability
> Forensic Interface Damage Manual

Integrity: building envelope interfaces when using multiple modern materials.
> Achievable economic lifetime durability of building envelopes

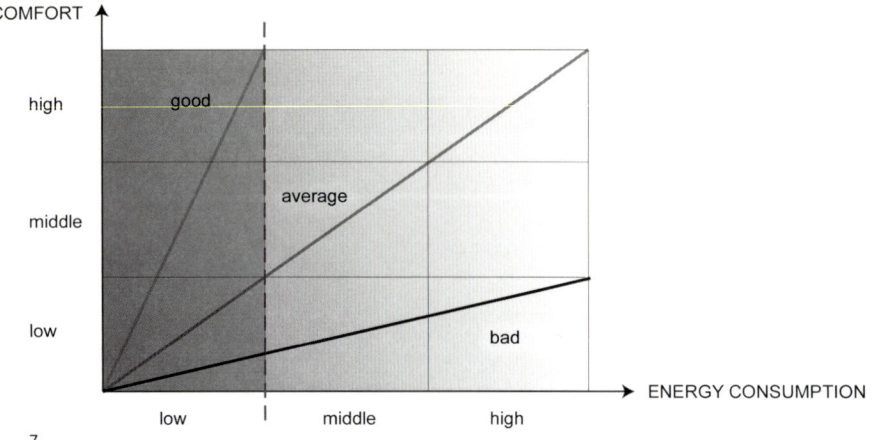

COMFORT

high — good

middle — average

low — bad

ENERGY CONSUMPTION

low · middle · high

7

8

9

---

7 The aim: to dissociate comfort from energy consumption

8 Atrium as buffer zone (Shanghai Tobacco Building, Shanghai China)

9 Currently, facades show various forms of energy optimization, responding flexibly to microclimate and macroclimate changes by using moveable vacuum panels as temporary thermal insulation.
on the right: Photovoltaic elements as part of the design (Schüco E² facade)

Building Physics: Zero-carbon building envelopes with fully optimized or integrated building services.

› Low-carbon building envelopes for minimal building services
› Intelligent and adaptive total building envelopes

Innovation

Considered over their whole life cycle, innovative building envelopes minimize unnecessary and unproductive consumption of energy, material, money, and time. In addition to energy-efficient and material-efficient concepts and products, this requires highly efficient planning, construction, and operation processes. The viability of the problem-solving approach increases if the system boundaries are extended. Truly innovative solutions (for both new buildings and existing ones) do not stop at considering the building envelope – they look at the building and all its components, together with its immediate and wider surroundings, extending to the traffic of people and items. They provide for the interconnection of the individual buildings within extensive buffer zones ("islands") with climate-effective envelopes suited to the location and with a regenerative energy supply. However, they also link the building and electric vehicles into a regional transport net. The aim is to maximize the length of time during which both comfortable living and working conditions capable of meeting changing requirements and individual mobility are ensured within the "island" without needing to import resources. This problem-solving approach is based on the efficiency strategy and depends on the optimal conversion and

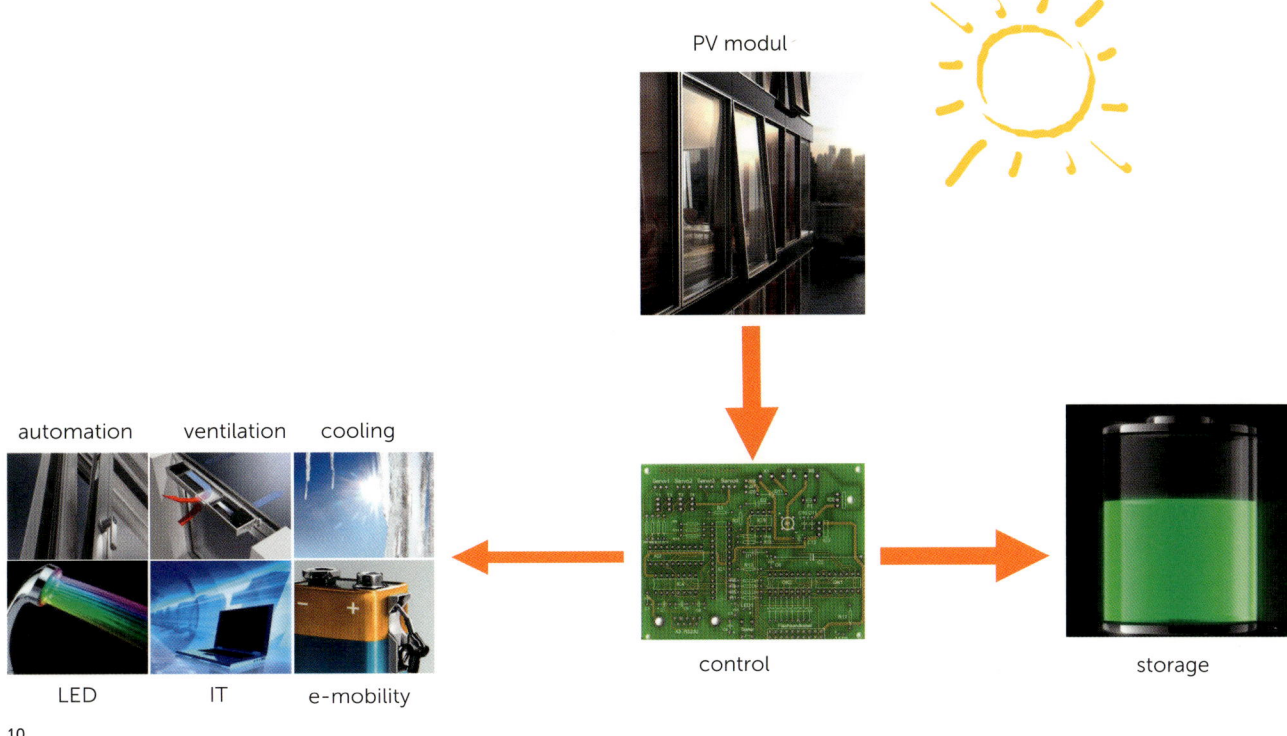

PV modul

automation   ventilation   cooling

control

storage

LED   IT   e-mobility

10

10 Connection system for
energy-producing and energy-
consuming components
(Schüco E^3 principle)

use of finite natural resources. Its success determines the ecological and economic success of the concept.

To enable these complex requirements for buildings and building envelopes the planning disciplines, in the form of architects, designers, engineers, and contractors, must be prepared. Architects supported by more multidisciplinary knowledge capital will be able to specify facade engineering solutions that reflect more accurately their design aspirations with less complex decision-making processes and improved clarity. At the same time these solutions contribute significantly to sustainability over the life cycle of the building.

It is possible that now, at the end of the third wave of globalization, the time is right for a global, sustainable network of "islands" that are largely independent in terms of resources. Innovative, climate-efficient climate envelopes function simultaneously as a semipermeable membrane and as collective services for the regenerative energy supply, making them an integral part of a sustainable regional plan. In some countries, it may be advisable to combine the climate concept with a security concept (with barriers, surveillance cameras, and security staff). The shared tasks, then, include – aside from the reliable provision of a sustainable infrastructure – possibly also the construction and operation of the climate envelopes, including its maintenance: in other words, guaranteeing a moderated and secure island climate. This allows individuals to create their own energy-efficient and comfortable indoor climate in their immediate environment.

Engineers Construct Art

Thomas Henriksen

"I have created a space that can almost be said to erase the boundary between inside and outside – a place where you become a little uncertain as to whether you have stepped into a work of art or into part of the museum."

Olafur Eliasson

Vision

"Your Rainbow Panorama" walkway is a work of art by Olafur Eliasson, erected on top of the ARoS art museum in Aarhus, Denmark. Studio Olafur Eliasson (SOE) won the tendered design competition in 2006 and the project was executed from in 2007–2011. At the concept design stage SOE worked with ArtEngineering to design the glass components of the supporting structure. The project was built by Rohlfing Stahlbau.

The work of art enters into a dialogue with the existing architecture, and blurs the lines between art and architecture, inside and outside. The view toward the city is constantly changed by the colored reflections and the movement of the visitor, encouraging him or her to question common boundaries and experiences. The installation "Your Rainbow Panorama" consists of an inner and outer glass ring that produce a rainbow effect, since each panel in the walkway has its own transparent color. The walkway is 52m in diameter, consisting of 58 different panels in each ring, and is elevated 4m above the roof of the museum. Each glass element of the circular skywalk has another transparent color and contributes to the intended rainbow effect. The view is not disturbed by any construction elements as the glass is the primary structural element that

1

1 Walkway, interior view,
© Thilo Frank/Studio Olafur
Eliasson

supports the roof of the walkway and acts as a stiffening element for the box girder. The greatest challenge in implementing the artist's design was the consistent use in construction of the colored glass as the essential element for the appearance of the installation.

Method

Glass and steel interaction

All steps in the planning process were thus reviewed in consideration of the design and the intended appearance. The glass is colored using a Saflex interlayer with the Vanceva color system, and has up to four different colored layers per panel to achieve the right tone. The principles of the technical design concept, particularly the interaction of the steel structure with the glass panels, have been investigated and verified using different Finite Element (FE) models. Personal safety, fire resistance, load-bearing capacity, and the glass manufacturer's capabilities were the parameters governing the dimensioning of the glass panels. The walkway consists of five main structural parts:

> roof of the walkway
> structural curved glass walls
> steel box girder
> 14 columns that lift the walkway 4m above the roof (spaced at max. 20m)
> the load-distributing beam system, which transfers the loads from the walkway columns to the ARoS building

2

Initially it was envisioned that the glass would be decoupled from the bottom box girder. However, at the interface between the glass and the steel no solution was found that would completely decouple the glass. The glass thus interacts with the box girder, providing additional stiffness to the structural system. This made extra requirements of the glass because of the long span between the fourteen supporting columns of the box girder. The wind load was the governing factor determining the glass dimensions. The force on the lower half of the glass is transferred directly to the box girder, and on the upper half to the roof plate of the walkway. The glass panels behave as single spanning beam elements with a slight membrane effect. The roof plate acts as an arch and transfers the localized wind loads to the sides of the walkway and down to the box girder by relatively small shear and normal forces through the glass.

The concept design was verified by the construction company and its consultants. As mentioned, the support condition of the glass was changed under the detailed design. The new structural concept was verified using an FE program. The authority approval presented additional requirements for the structural use of glass: it had to withstand an impact load at the same time as snow and wind load. Overall deflections are shown in Fig. 8.

Selection of the glass

The use of structural glass to transfer the loads of a roof structure has featured recently in several buildings such as The Crypt entrance to Saint Martin in the Fields in London (designed by Eric Perry and engineered by Arup). The glass

3

4

3 Walkway, exterior view,
© Thilo Frank/Studio Olafur
Eliasson

4 Walkway, exterior view,
© Thilo Frank/Studio Olafur
Eliasson

must be capable of transferring vertical loads and the bending moments, to ensure stability of the glass and the roof. Additional requirements must be fulfilled before permitting the use of structural glass as a primary load-bearing material:

> The glass must be safety glass and fulfill class 2B2 in EN12600 [53].
> The glass must fulfill the requirement of a class A1 material.
> The load-bearing elements in the walkway must resist fire for 60 minutes (F60) and seal the walkway from the ingress of smoke.
> The glass must have sufficient strength and stiffness to accommodate the loads.

The new walkway has an outer diameter of 26m in such a way that the walkway meets the building's edge (52 × 52m in plan) at four positions. The 4m difference between the walkway and the building's roof requires the glass to be laminated to meet the safety-glass criteria in local building regulations [54]. The glass is class A1 and it is not flammable. However, the 60 minutes' fire resistance (F60 – highly fire retardant) requirement can only be met if a fire insulating material is used in combination with the glass such that it retains its structural integrity when subjected to direct flames. Consequently, this makes it difficult to use colored interlayers in the glass and is not an acceptable solution to the Studio of Olafur Eliasson. Instead, a solution was derived from investigating the probability of a fire with open flames on the walkway. It was shown that by adding sprinklers and ensuring that inflammable material is used on the roof a probable fire would not have a magnitude great enough for open flames to reach the

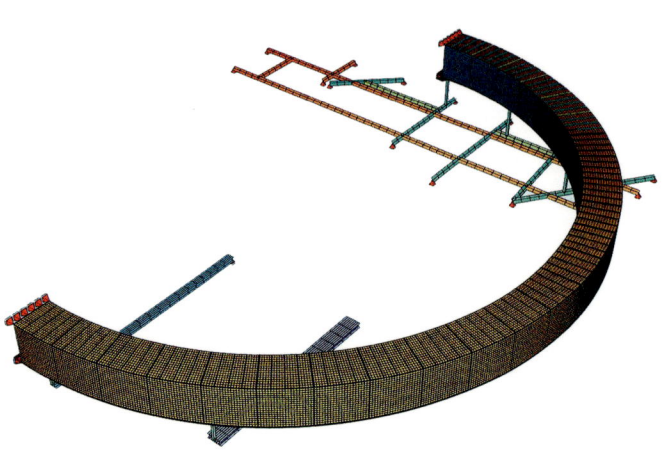

5

6

---

5 FE model of the walkway
structure with load-distributing
beams, © ArtEngineering

6 Section of the walkway,
© Thilo Frank/Studio Olafur
Eliasson

glass. The smoke would have a temperature exceeding 350°C when it touches the glass. The glass therefore needs to be heat-treated, toughened, or heat-strengthened. Previous tests showed that 2 × 12mm heat-strengthened glass would accommodate smoke of up to 450°C before the glass laminate starts to disintegrate. Two layers of toughened glass could potentially lose their combined structural integrity after a fracture. Therefore two layers of heat-strengthened glass or a mix of heat-strengthened and toughened glass would have the best performance in a fire.

The structural requirements for the glass were derived from the imposed loadings using Eurocode 1 [55]. The loadings applied to the dimensioning glass pane are as follows (vertical loads have been disregarded): Wind load: 1.59kN/m² (pressure) and 1.15kN/m² (suction) applied perpendicularly to the glass surface. The maximum stresses in the glass were calculated using an FE model as part of the structural model. The allowable design stresses for the glass were determined according to prEN14373-3 [56].

The curved glass panels are 3.2m high and 2.8m wide and consist of two 12mm leaves of glass laminated together. Additional parameters must be considered when selecting the glass composition: the usages of colored interlayer, post-breakage integrity, and production capabilities. The colored interlayer in the glass could potentially accumulate heat, and since the top and bottom of the panel are hidden in a frame there could be a risk of thermal breakage in the glass, if annealed glass is used. This means that the glass must be heat-treated, as annealed glass cannot fulfill the requirements. Experience from other glass

7

7 Computer model of the
walkway, © ArtEngineering

structures shows that the usages of two layers of toughened glass can collapse under its own weight if both panes are broken; therefore using glass with different break patterns is preferred [57]. If both layers are broken, the different break patterns keep the glass intact and will have sufficient capacity to work as a barrier against impact.

If two leaves of toughened glass would be considered, structural silicone would be used to keep them intact. Hot fumes could reduce the silicone's stiffness and result in the glass collapsing. The suggested glass composition in this situation is a combination of heat-strengthened glass and toughened glass. The heat-strengthened glass should be placed on the inside of the walkway to prevent it from breaking if small impact damages are made to the glass. The preferred solution would be 12mm heat-strengthened + 12mm toughened glass, laminated together with colored PVB interlayers. However, due to geometric differences in the production of the curved toughened glass and heat-strengthened glass this was not possible to produce, and 2 × 12mm toughened glass was produced instead (by Sunglass). The strategy was that if both leaves are broken, an intermediate support replaces the glass, as the roof panels can carry the broken glass until the temporary support is in place.

The optical quality of the glass is also significant as the glass is used as part of a work of art and is a panoramic viewpoint. Since curved glass has been seen to have bad optical quality, it was specified that the glass supplier only use an oscillating furnace to bend the glass.

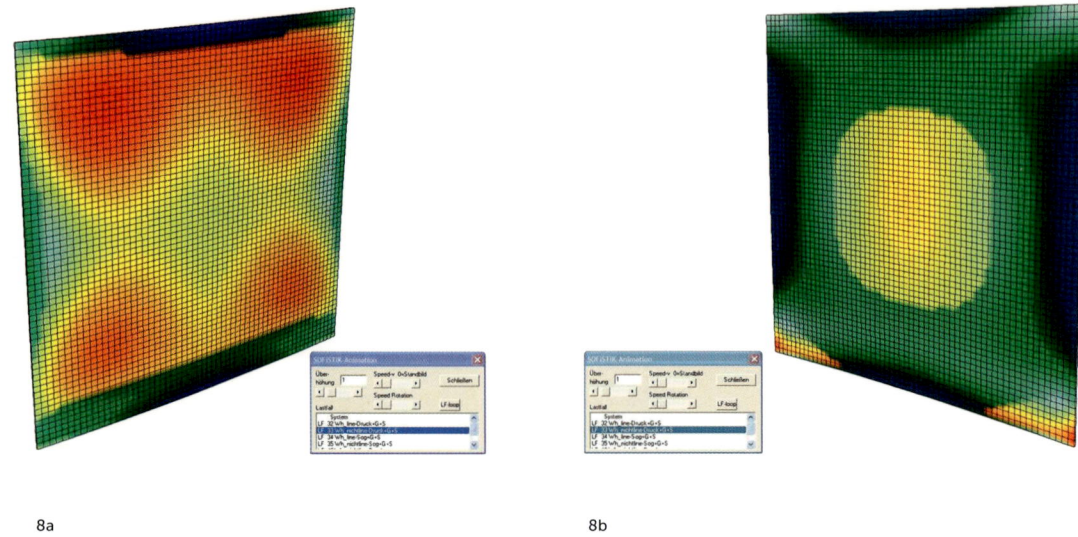

8a   8b

8a,b Stress plot of curved glass,
© ArtEngineering

Finally the curved glass was tested according to CWCT technical note TN66 and Tn67 [58] to ensure satisfactory performance. Four specimens were given soft- and hard-body impact tests and a wind load test using sandbags as the imposed loading. Several wind load tests were undertaken for the glass; with both leaves intact, one leaf broken and both leaves broken.

Innovation

The walkway "Your Rainbow Panorama" is the first of its kind in Denmark in an area accessible by the public. The usage of structural glass was approved by the municipality of Aarhus and the walkway was officially opened in May 2011. The greatest challenge for implementation was the overlay of numerous extreme requirements made by the artist, the construction itself, and the regulator. The resolution of these sometimes contradictory requirements resulted from an iterative planning and optimization process, which produced a convincing solution in this interaction between art and engineered construction [59].

9

9 Walkway, panoramic view,
© Thilo Frank/Studio Olafur
Eliasson

Expanding
_____
Networks

Open Innovation

Eckard Foltin
Lorenz Kramer
Holger Strauß

Vision

Innovation can be successful only if we look to tomorrow's needs today. Open innovation is a strategy pursued by companies in collaboration with experts from outside, in order to design development processes that are close to practice and to clients, and to do justice to the dynamism of the framework conditions. The early involvement of partners from the value-added chain enables development goals to be implemented more rapidly [60].

Bayer MaterialScience AG (BMS) has been actively supporting the setting up of an open innovation network to develop application concepts for lifestyle, home and work, under the name future_bizz. Within the network, experts from industry meet researchers and academics, and connect the cutting edge of research with the current state of technology. The Hochschule Ostwestfalen-Lippe (HS OWL), with its departments of architecture, interior architecture and design, has been a member of this network for several years.

Method

Network projects are initiated to work through a focus topic within a defined period: for example, to formulate a market demand as a vision. Starting from a more general task specification, concrete project goals and the necessary project participants are defined. In a joint briefing for all project participants, the plan and the target expectations are articulated in the context of the available

1

background information. After discussion, the procedure in the project and a schedule are agreed.

The project Click & GO was undertaken jointly between BMS and students of the HS OWL in the master's program International Facade Design and Construction (IFDC). The students all have expertise in building but, as an intercultural technical team of experts, process the topic with their different perspectives and skills. This diversity of the master's students was intended to spark new approaches, particularly in the area of building insulation, as the participants approached the topic with highly varied backgrounds and experience in building culture and design.

To drive the creative process, the specific cooperation between business and teaching enabled the product search to be targeted, market-relevant, and use the latest specialist knowledge. This interweaving of realistic figures and requirements and the creative freedom of teaching and of the students led to the shared development of deepened understanding and learning.

Market conditions and the principles of market logic were taught by Gerd Daffertshofer, an experienced and independent external coach with many years of marketing experience.

The project leadership lay with the BMS Creative Center, and specific topics were taught by the material, technology, and application experts from the business areas. The focus was on polyurethane foams, the heat-insulating materials that reach the optimum values.

2

3

2 Brainstorming

3 Concept finding

The project Click & GO applied the market pull approach in the open innovation process, developing in stages to extend an initial idea into a potential innovation and thus a future product. The procedure and development criteria will be described below using examples.

Briefing

As a basis for the independent development of new ideas, the available materials, technologies, possible markets, and existing applications for the PU materials were first presented. The working title "Click & GO" refers to the ease of use of the new applications, and also expresses the possibility of a future use of insulation that is not just static, but can adapt dynamically to climatic changes that take place over the course of a day or a year.

Materials collection

Through the joint orientation, the market situation was determined using a market study of the insulation materials that are available, in use, or new. The international markets and globally available products for building insulation were analyzed, so that the market relevance of the ideas that arose could always be determined. This is necessary in order to recognize potentials among a multiplicity of ideas, using market-relevant factors. Only approaches that will later be in demand on the market can be developed as innovations.

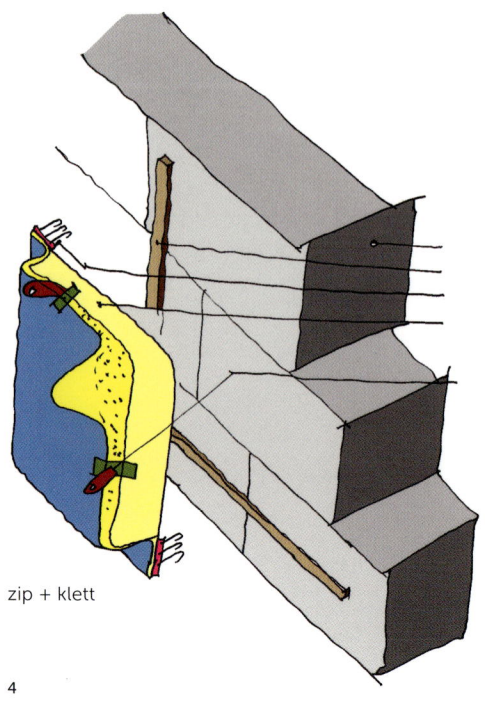

zip + klett

4

4 Zip-Klett by Barbara Hyska

Generation of ideas

For the technological basis of today's PU insulation products, we sketched and formulated initial ideas with the participants in a creative workshop [61]. In the team discussion the mixture of technological and economic background knowledge, combined with the students' fresh views on the desired performance of a future heat insulation system, led to the generation of holistic, forward-looking concepts.

Checking market needs and sketching a dream concept as a possible solution

From the product research we can state that the market for insulating materials will grow in the decade up to 2020. A large share of this market will be home users, who will make their own efforts to reduce their energy consumption through insulation. To be attractive to these customers the products must be varied and simple to use (for example, the Click-and-Go principle for floors or wall coverings). One idea has been to link a well-known product (Velcro) with variable insulating panels. This dream concept offers the possibility of modular facade insulation that can be adapted to the funds available and to any structural modifications. Its use must be intuitive, and later upgrades possible.

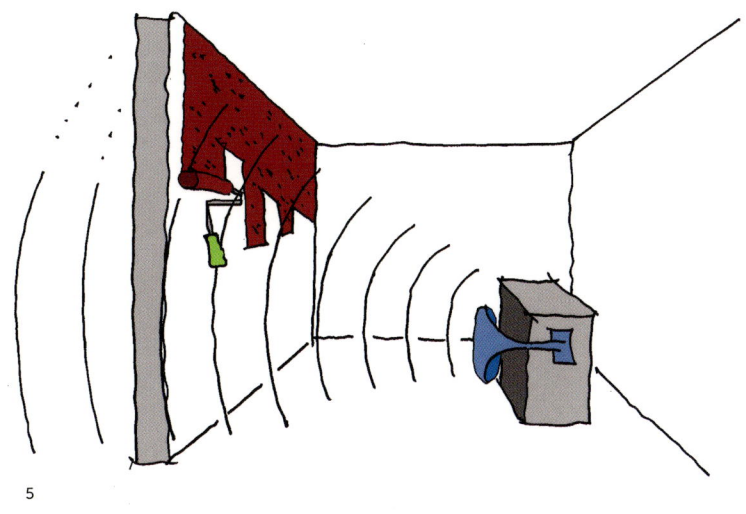

5

5 PU sound insulation by
Hemant Yadav

Added value and unique selling points

In processing, it becomes clear that a future market could offer two starting points: lower costs for the user, or improved product characteristics. The second point was the focus of the creative process, as actual costs can only be determined in a later study. The result was the development of a new application of the surface expansion and sound-insulating properties of PU as a material: an active wall covering that improves sound insulation and is as simple to use as a conventional wall paint.

Recognizing usefulness to customers; sustainable system solutions through process optimization

The linkage of different disciplines – in this case construction engineering and architecture – transformed the need for simply erectable structures into a further idea for structural planning: PU in forms that can easily be reduced in size for transport, and equipped with an internal self-foaming support structure. In its later use on the building, the combination of lightweight framework and pneumatic structure offers a hybrid solution for roofs.

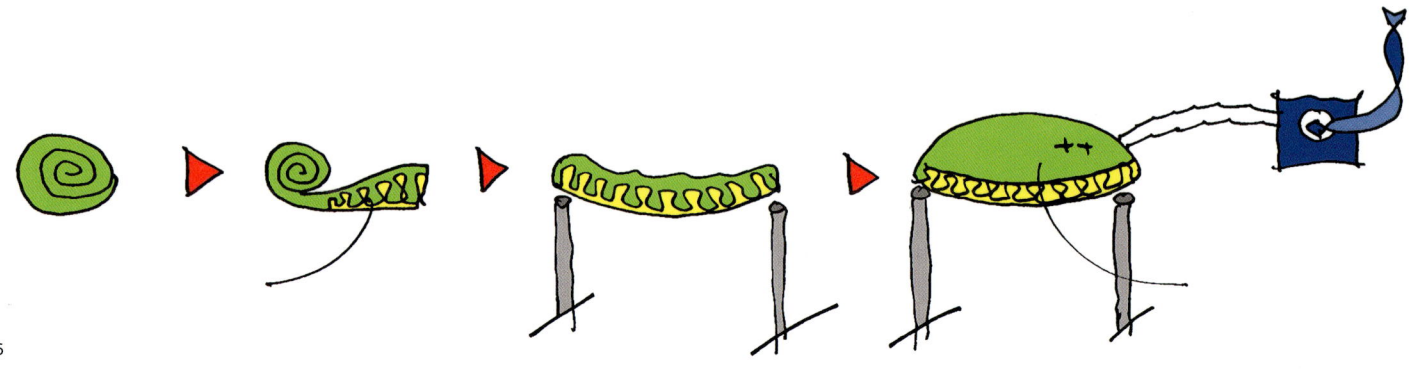

6

6 Pneumatic PU structures by
Surachat Gumngen

Presenting a business opportunity

Innovative concepts also require a strategy for turning them into a business model. This strategy describes the steps in which the market may develop, and the chance of implementation can be analyzed in the value-added chain. At the start of the project, a market segmentation analysis was carried out, and the potential of the different insulating materials evaluated. The system solutions with polyurethane produced by the process show the development potential for these markets. For instance, they target possible innovations in shaping, insulation of thin walls, simplification of fitting, and alternative distribution channels.

Innovation

In order to place new products on the market – made by an innovative process – and generate additional growth outside of current business, new solutions are needed in which cooperation and teamwork are important components. Lone wolves and isolated applications no longer provide this service. The open innovation approach demonstrates one way of accelerating development processes through interdisciplinary exchange, and deriving new business opportunities from ideas.

7 "Tranquility Flooring" by
Hemant Yadav

Connections and Layers

Christoph Kirch
Thomas Böhm

Idea and Vision

Small to medium-sized enterprises (SMEs) in the building sector are normally different from companies that are classically featured in research. Many of these companies have their origins in the trade, like Böhm GmbH, or are founded on a patent, like SilenceSolutions GmbH. In their day-to-day handling of various construction-related tasks, they are constantly confronted with the need to optimize existing products, to adapt to changing demands, or to break into new markets and niches. This makes it necessary, in economic terms, to implement a targeted product development strategy even if the company has no in-house research department. In this respect, these two companies chose a different path: Böhm GmbH cooperated with several research institutes, and SilenceSolutions GmbH opted to collaborate with a university in a publicly funded program.

After conducting research, Böhm GmbH ascertained that there were no large-format ceramic facade elements currently on the market. The starting point for the firm's in-house development process was a large-format 3mm-thick high-tech ceramic element with a variety of coatings depending on its area of intended use, marketed under the brand name VidroStone®. The material is used in museums, shops, hotels, and private interiors. It possesses exceptional mechanical properties and can be worked to highly specific parameters.

SilenceSolutions has already possessed the rights to an innovative and patented multilayered sound absorption system of flexible polyurethane foam (PUR),

1 Apartment in Berlin.
Application: furnishings,
floor and wall surfaces,
bath, terrace, LED lights,
fireplace mantle

called a multi-impedance absorber. This kind of absorbent material is highly effective and able to absorb the whole frequency spectrum (wide-band absorption). Due to its particularly high effectiveness in the low-frequency range, it also possesses a significantly flatter construction than conventional porous absorbers. Because it uses PUR, however, this system does not comply with the more exacting fire protection standards for public facilities. The multilayer principle therefore had to be adapted for nonflammable class A fire protection materials. The market has previously offered few nonflammable materials or products with good absorption properties. The publicly funded project was concerned with the analysis of these materials and with sound absorber development. In addition to acoustic standards, commercial and public buildings must also satisfy high standards in terms of aesthetics and comfort. A functional design analysis of the existing absorbers showed that a more modular design was required so that the surface could be altered to create solutions tailored to a variety of applications.

Method

In both cases, interactions between different specialist areas and interdisciplinary collaborations involving physical scientific analysis and space design skills played a role. In the case of Böhm GmbH, thought exercises and exchanges with a wide variety of people – during work time and free time – took place throughout every stage of the development process. Initially, there was a discussion only within the inner circle of this family business. Subsequently, external contacts

2

3

2 Jewish Museum Berlin –
Foyer

3 Glass cases, NOESA Beautycare
Shop in Seoul, Korea

and advice became extremely important for ensuring an expedient developmental process. Relevant disciplines included physics and chemistry (with particular note to adhesive technology), marketing and law, funding options, and official and administrative procedures. This complex interdisciplinary networking and research process required confidentiality. Internally, this was implemented by means of IT infrastructure; externally, it was achieved through design protection, agreements, and patents. The research process for the facade elements extended over seven years and incorporated a variety of procedures and combinations of different materials, which produced additional innovations. For instance, a special low-emission adhesive material with no evaporation was developed for museum buildings to protect sensitive exhibits. The aim was also to develop a new adhesive and bonding technology for the facade panel. Due to reasons of weight, it could not be glued to a glass plate in the inner area as had previously been the case; instead, it was to be combined with a lightweight construction material and a simple fastening technology.

Right at the outset, a formal framework was established for the SilenceSolutions GmbH research project, with the phases of work on the project determined in advance. The search for suitable absorption and surface materials that would satisfy fire protection and damping requirements and the process of comparison with products in current use was carried out on a number of levels:

> Open-ended research of specialist literature, material databases, and manufacturers' information allows products already on the market to be selected

4

5

---

4 Layer thickness and layer construction of the ceramic elements for interiors

5 Existing sound absorption systems for use in office premises.

> The "Detmolder GreifBar" materials library, which includes approximately 350 innovative products, gives a reliable impression of the current state of development of raw materials

> The "CES EduPack" is a toolkit for raw materials and processing technologies in science and development, providing supplementary and comparison information on materials' technical, economic, and environmental properties. The results are expressed in materials charts, which provide an overview of the parameters in diagram form.

A table was compiled giving the results of data gathered in this way for 49 materials and products, grouped in a number of categories: glass foam, natural stone (expanded/fibre-form minerals), metal foam, and worked stone (mineral foam). In addition to this, material patterns were assessed and evaluated. Alongside porosity, flammability, and projected absorption properties, price was a key factor: metal foams, for instance, were unfeasible due to high costs. As none of the low-flammability materials achieved the same low values as PUR foam ($50kg/m^3$), compromises had to be reached on strength and, in particular, on bulk density.

In the age of Internet search engines, numerous materials databanks, and other service providers, it should in theory be easy to track down and select the most suitable materials. However, it quickly becomes clear how differently materials are represented and presented in each of the different branches and sectors of the industries concerned. Not all of the required information was easily obtained from the manufacturers, and materials were often categorized according to properties that did not facilitate direct comparison.

6

6 The "GreifBar" materials library
at the Hochschule OWL

Once this research had been conducted, it was necessary to make additional comparative measurements of the core and surface materials in order to ensure a reliable basis for comparison and to obtain the missing acoustic parameters. Following a preliminary selection based on sampling and impedance tube measurements, the materials' and coatings' various degrees of sound absorption were determined using a reverberation chamber [62]. Various material combinations and layer thicknesses were tested until, ultimately, the same positive results associated with the flammable PUR foam were achieved by combining mineral wools with different high-bulk densities. At this point, the most crucial goal – to replace the flammable absorbent material used in the existing absorber with a nonflammable core material possessing the same acoustic values – had been attained.

The functional design development process began with a typological investigation of the application and integration of the absorber modules in typical indoor situations. Architectonic design issues made it desirable to be able to emphasize or efface the modules as necessary, enhancing the absorber modules with higher-quality surface materials and edge/join details, and integrating the absorber modules into construction components.

The surface material determines the absorbers' appearance, their value, and their capabilities for integration into the interior design [63]. To allow sound to penetrate the absorber, a percentage of its surface area must be made open (by means of perforations, for instance). Research and metrological tests re-

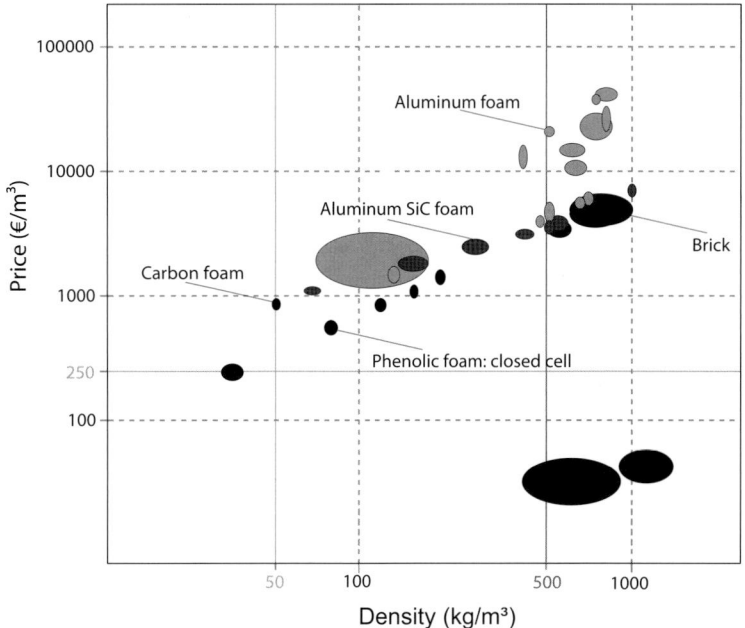

Price / Density
Stage 3
Limit: Nonflammable, less than 1000 Kg/m³

7

7 CES EduPack materials chart: price to bulk density of core materials

vealed that the most suitable surface materials [64] in acoustic and design terms were: glass fibre fabric, fine wire mesh, expanded metal, and perforated sheet metal.

Results

At construction level, the absorber modules under development would need to perform a number of functions simultaneously. The project succeeded in developing a new aluminum extruded-profile frame system to allow these functions. Primarily, the frame provided static scaffolding for the absorption material, which possessed low inherent strength and solidity. The surface materials, with mechanical properties that varied widely, also had to be incorporated into the construction of the absorber modules. A convenient tensioning/clamping system was developed for the fabrics, with the fabric clipped into a groove by means of an aluminum rod in order to secure it and keep it stretched. The perforated plates and expanded metal elements, which are more rigid, were secured in the constructions as filling. They are interchangeable: any acoustic materials that are rigid enough to hold the absorber core in place while forming the outward-facing surface of the frame-filling element can be used.

The design of the perforated sheet metal surface materials was changed to improve them and to make them useable in a number of areas. Ornamental designs were developed, created by means of additional perforations in the

Acoustic absorption in comparison

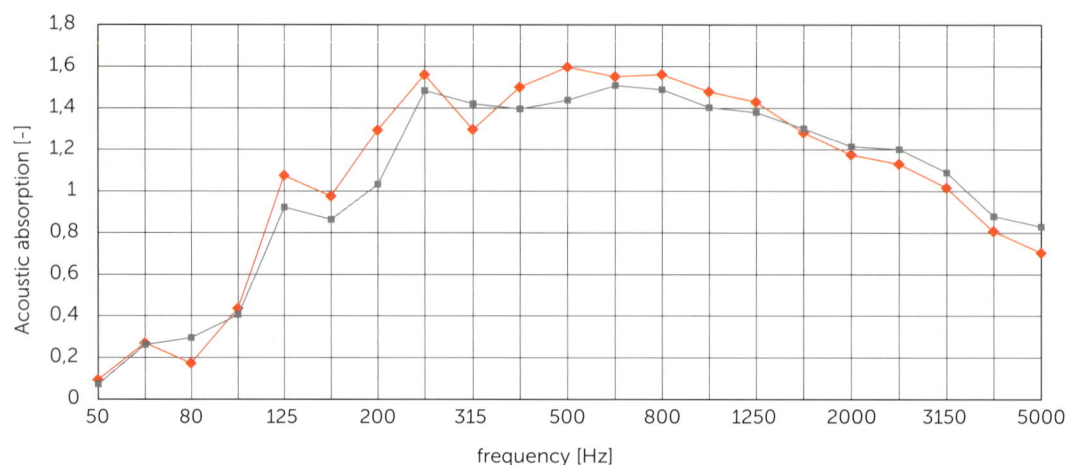

8   9

◆ New, nonflammable system: mineral wool layered inside the acoustic panel
■ Existing system: PUR layered inside the acoustic panel

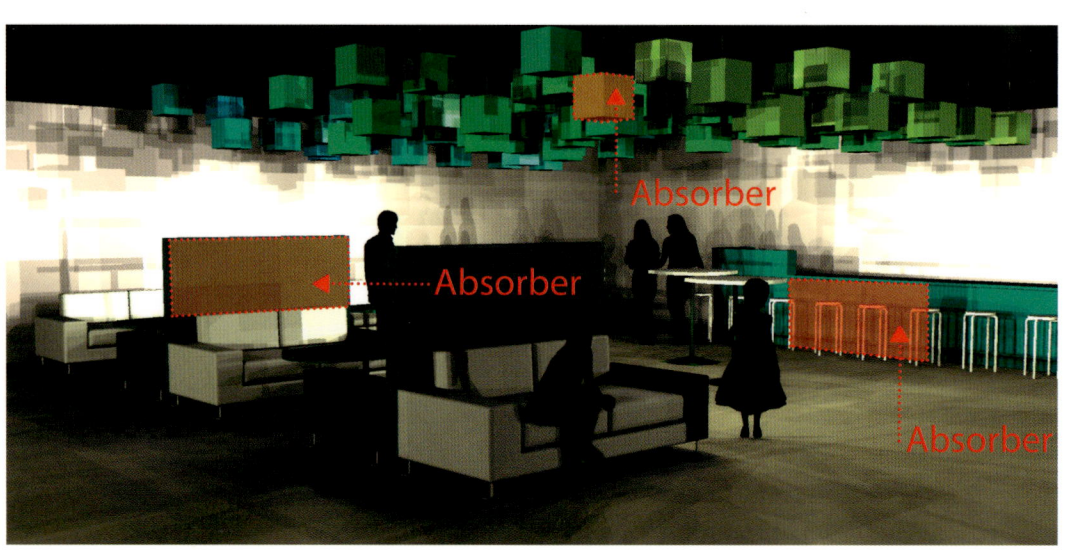

10

8 Layering of materials for acoustic tests

9 Comparison of measurement results: the nonflammable module compared to the existing PUR module

10 Application and integration of the absorber modules in an indoor situation

11

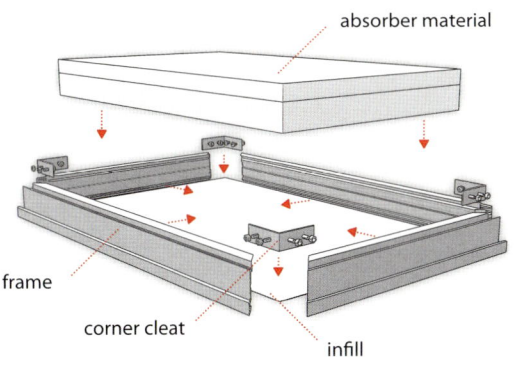

12

frame

corner cleat

infill

absorber material

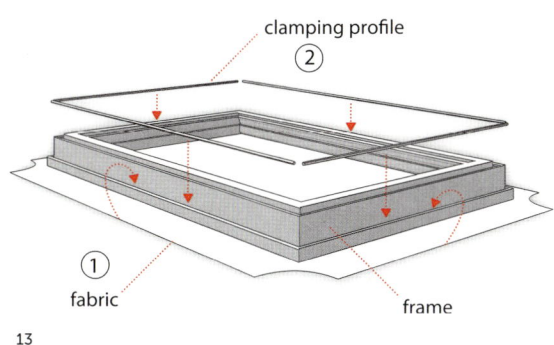

13

clamping profile

②

①

fabric

frame

11 Surface materials: expanded
metal, perforated sheet metal,
glass and metal mesh

12 Construction principles
of the frame system for the
absorber module

13 The clip system used to
secure the fabric surfaces.

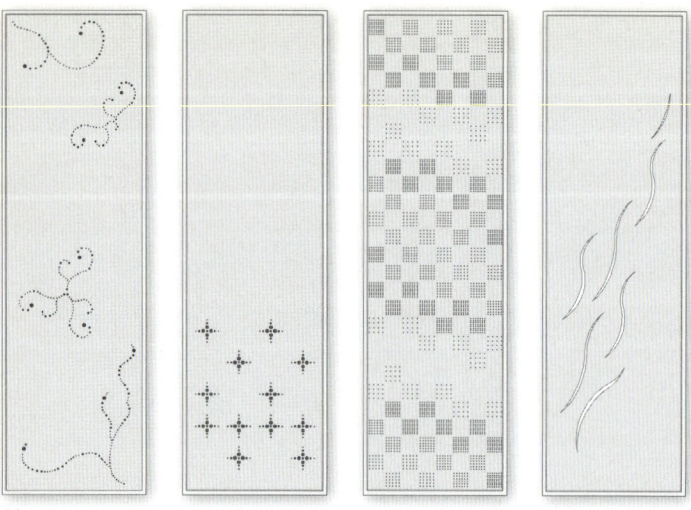

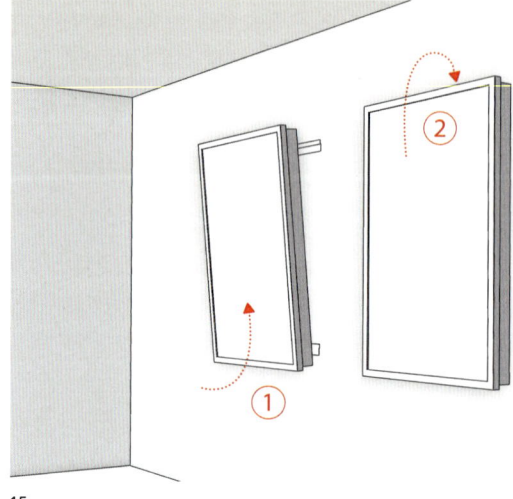

14 Perforated sheet metal
surfaces embellished with
ornamental perforations

15 Mounting principle for
wall module

sheet metal. This can be used as filling in the frame profile, but can also be used for the existing system. The acoustic module had to be suitable for mounting on the wall or the ceiling and also suitable for integration into architectonic components. To facilitate this, the profile was fitted with a mounting system for the ceiling and wall.

The plan also included a monoblock separating wall module compatible with the existing glass separating wall system. A clip system was developed for this purpose that allowed two similar modules to be joined together by a connecting profile to create a separating wall module. These elements are fitted into a ceiling and floor profile like a glass pane. This expedites on-site mounting by avoiding the time-consuming assemblage of many small individual parts, pedestal profiles, and glass retainer profiles.

Böhm GmbH has achieved a facade panel with maximum measurements of 3.60×1.24m by combining the large, industrially produced ceramic elements with a suitably light carrier material. It is weather-resistant and fireproof, and therefore has a long useful life. The large-format elements keep the proportion of joints to a minimum, creating an exceptional surface quality, which is desirable and the subject of considerable demand from architects and clients. The specialized point-fixed subconstruction of the individual ceramic elements creates a back-ventilated facade construction. A weight of 25kg/m^2 and an integrated anchorage system facilitates mounting onsite. This avoids adaptation work: no additional cuts or positioning are required to create a backcut system onsite.

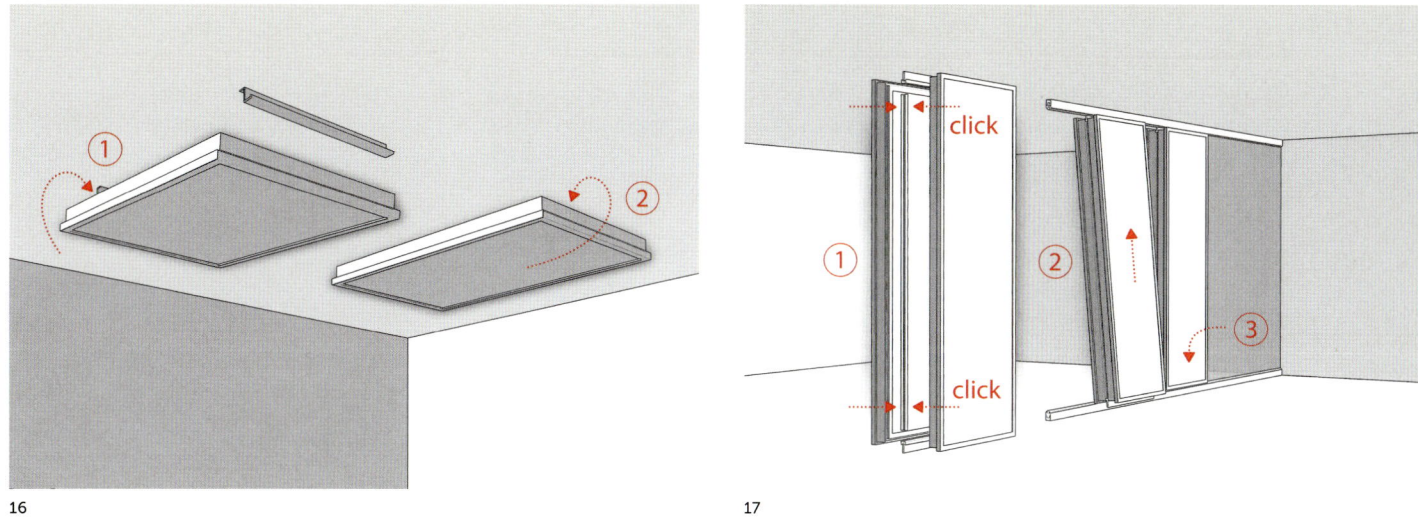

16   click   click   17

16   Mounting principle for ceiling module

17   Mounting principle for absorber separating wall module

In both cases, existing products were successfully modified, expanded, and applied to new areas. One striking aspect of these two projects is that reference standards for new developments and refinements of existing advancements were initiated and defined by the design and function requirements of the market.

Innovation

The sound absorption system's aluminum frame profile allowed the design and constructive integration to be extended and improved. An appealing visual appearance well adapted to usage conditions and integration with other construction components significantly increases flexibility and user acceptance. The new product has the advantage of being a flat system construction for a multilayer absorption system that is highly effective across the bandwidth for areas with increased fire protection requirements. In the case of the facade panel, as well, the combination of individual components to create a new product, with the addition of a simplified mounting system enabled by the integrated anchorage system and maximized prefabrication, constitutes an innovation.

There is no end in sight to the research and development process; instead, these refinements and optimizations will provide the foundation for future successes. In the future, it should be possible to deploy the absorber modules

19

20

18 Facade view, showing large-format 3.60 × 1.24 m panels

19 Facade construction

20 Anchorage system integrated into the facade panel

in combination with a sound-masking system [65]. For the facade panel, interactions with solar heating and solar power are being investigated. The real task – marketing – begins after the development process is complete. For medium-sized companies, this is a major financial and organizational challenge, particularly in our globalized age. A crucial factor here is whether market demand has been correctly assessed, and whether the product can break into new market sectors and regional markets.

21

22

21 Luxury apartment with sea
view project, India – general view

22 Luxury apartment with sea
view project, India – detail view

Conserving
Resources

Energy Supplying Envelope

Jan Wurm

Vision

Biomass and microalgae technology

Biomass is stored solar energy. One major benefit of using it as a fuel is that it can be stored with virtually no energy loss. Bioenergy accounts for the largest percentage of overall energy consumption of any form of renewable energy (7%); in Germany, it is the second most significant source of energy for electricity generation after wind energy. Biomass is available in solid (e.g., firewood or wood pellets), liquid (e.g., biodiesel) or gaseous form (biogas), and can be used in a highly flexible way in the fields of electricity generation, heat generation, and fuel production. Obtaining energy from biomass is a CO_2-neutral process because burning releases the same amount of carbon dioxide into the atmosphere that was initially absorbed in its formation.

Their ability to efficiently convert sunlight into biomass makes microalgae one of the most promising building blocks for alternative energy scenarios today. Like other plants, microalgae use the sun as a source of energy, combining it with CO_2 and nutrients (nitrogen and phosphorus) to produce biomass. This photosynthesis process takes place in the same manner as it would in agricultural crops. Microalgae, however, convert light energy into biomass considerably more efficiently than higher plants because they are single-celled plants, with photosynthesis taking place in every individual cell.

	2008	2009	2010	2011	share building integrated 2011
biomass	125.000	144.000	160.500	163.390	0 %
wind power	40.500	38.500	36.500	46.500	0 %
water power	20.500	19.000	20.000	19.500	0 %
solar energy	8.600	11.000	17.000	24.600	3 %
geothermal	4.600	5.000	5.500	6.340	
sum	**199.200**	**204.000**	**239.500**	**260.330**	
share in gross power demand	9,3 %	10,2 %	11,3 %	12,2 %	

1

1 The contribution of renewable energy to power generation and heat generation in Germany [GWh] – source: renewable energy report, Federal Ministry of Environment, Natural Protection and Reactor Savety (BMU) 2011

Unlike the cultivation of energy crops such as maize, the cultivation of micro-algae does not take up additional land and therefore does not compete with the cultivation of food crops, and there is no dependence on weathering factors or need for intensive livestock farming. Microalgae can be cultivated in photobio-reactors (PBR). These are enclosed hollow bodies filled with a culture medium that are permeable to light, which can be installed in locations where conditions would be too dry or too harsh for other methods – such as in the center of a major city.

Bioreactive facade

Previously, the energy benefits of integrating tube collectors into facades have been canceled out by the relatively high construction costs involved. Recently, however, the development and testing of panel bioreactors has led to a break-through in the economically viable cultivation and utilization of microalgae. The convection reactor developed by the firm Strategic Science Consult (SSC) in Hamburg in the TERM pilot project permits open-air use all year round in North-ern European climatic conditions, while also achieving production rates that are significantly higher than those of other reactor systems. In terms of the conver-sion of sunlight into biomass, the coefficient is between 5% and 8%. Automated process and system operation enables continuous cultivation with low mainte-nance costs.

The periodic conduction of pressurized air to the underside of the reactor cre-ates turbulence within the reactor, increasing the mixing of the culture medium

2

3

4

5

with the continual influx of flue gas (CO_2) and optimizing the supply of light to the algae. The high speed of the currents around the bioreactor's inner surfaces prevents deposits of algae and biological waste matter on them. The heat produced in the reactor by solar thermal effect must be removed in order to prevent overheating in the medium. In this respect, the reactor functions like a solar collector with a coefficient of approximately 40% – approximately equal to that of an open absorber.

The added value associated with the cultivation of microalgae in bioreactor facades attached to buildings is shown here:

> The biomass stores CO_2
> The biomass can be converted into methane (biogas) or hydrogen, thereby serving as a source of renewable energy
> As with a solar collector, heat is generated that can then be used within the building
> Bioreactors are multifunctional facade elements that are also capable of providing light protection, heat and cold protection, and sound protection.
> Bioreactors can also operate as aperture elements, facilitating the natural ventilation of the building

Photobioreactors cause 25–250g CO_2/m^2 per day to be stored as biomass. The harvested biomass can be converted into biogas (methane) on-site by means of hydrothermal conversion. One m^2 of reactor surface produces an average of 15g dry mass per day per year, which is equal to 2.7m^3 of methane. At a fuel

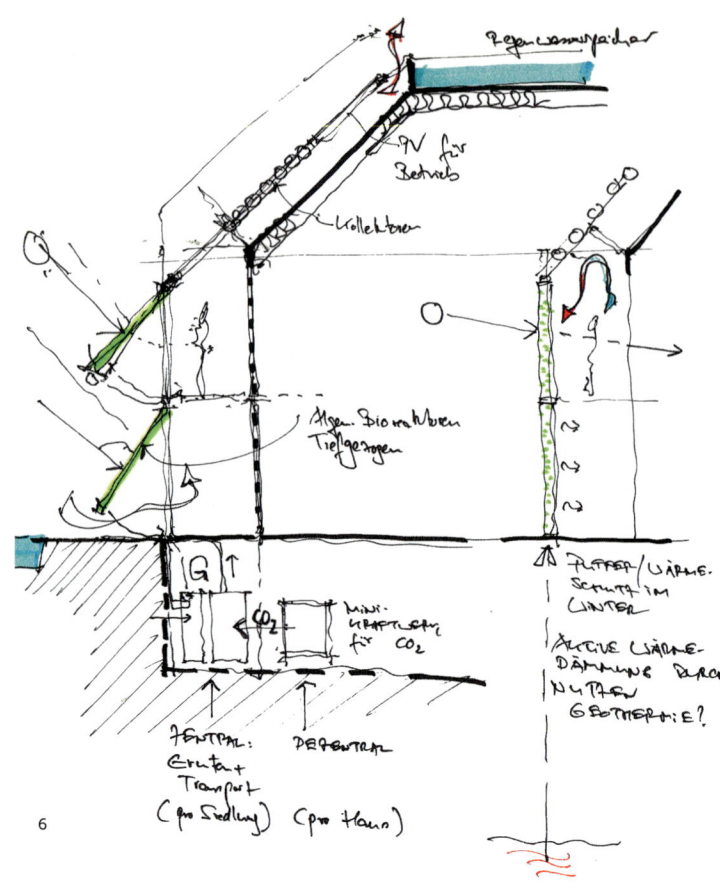

6

value of 10.6kWh/m of methane, a gross energy yield of approximately 29kWh/m²a can be achieved. The methane can be burned during the heating period, stored in the municipal natural gas grid, or used as engine fuel. By harnessing the solar thermal effect, a heat exchanger can increase the heat yield by approximately 30kWh/m²a. This can then be used for the hot-water supply by means of a heat pump. The auxiliary power supply for the systems and regulation technology is to be supplied directly by the PV modules.

Because the microalgae absorb light, PBR units also constitute effective sun-protection elements. The cell counts can be doubled or halved over the course of a day by harvesting the algae to thin them out or by suspending harvesting, permitting light permeability to be adjusted by 100%. In winter, reduced solar radiation reduces the algae content to only approximately 0.5g/l, resulting in a light permeability of over 30%. PBR can therefore replace traditional external sun-protection systems and collectors, while maintaining added value.

Method

Facade integration

The technology required for microalgae cultivation on buildings is shown in overview in Fig. 8. To ensure optimal lighting, the reactors are applied to the outer side of the facade as facade elements. The best orientation is from the southwest to the southeast. The load-bearing system with which the PBR is

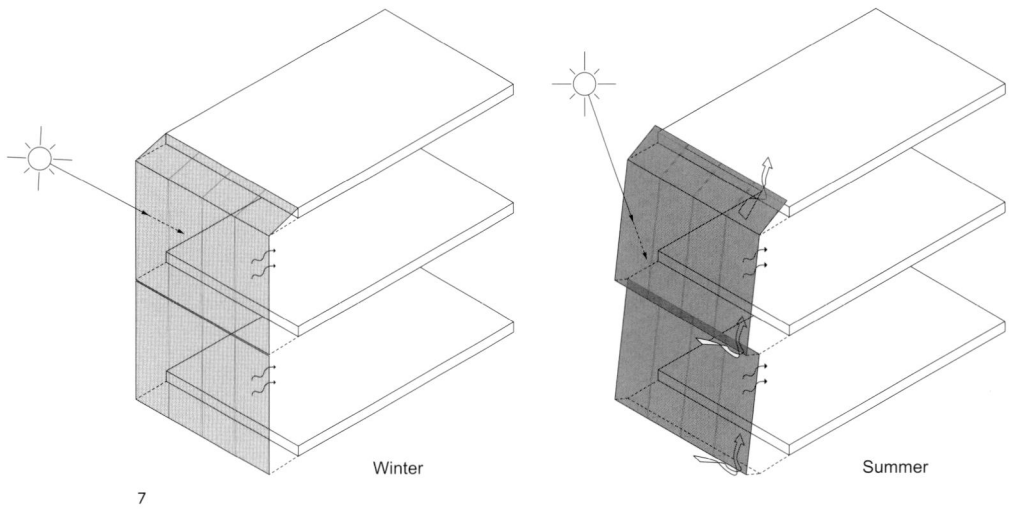

Winter

7

Summer

7 Schematic of the functioning
of the bioreactor facade in winter
and summer – the bioreactors
can be realigned in order to
facilitate natural ventilation or to
optimize orientation toward the
sun (reproduction: ©Arup GmbH)

secured to the facade, oriented and occasionally realigned is of primary importance. In the winter, a vertical positioning of the reactors creates a favorable
orientation due to the sun's low angle of incidence. In addition to this, where
there is no opening between the two, an air or buffer space between the PBR
and the thermal envelope can help to prevent heat loss. In summer, on the
other hand, turning the PBR to an angle of 30° from the level of a south facade
increases heat gain.

The bioreactors are connected in clusters of approximately 10m^2 in a row, so
that the medium circulates through all bioreactors. Sunlight causes the reactors
to additionally heat up over the course of a day; they function in the same way
as solar thermal absorbers. The heat and biomass are cycled via the in-building
systems, with both removed at a central point. The energy generated is stored
or distributed by means of the energy management center.

The heat is transferred through a heat exchanger in the in-buildings systems
room, and is then stored within or inside the structure of the building (floor plate
or PCM storage) or used directly to heat water. In winter, the operating temperature of the algae must not be allowed to sink below 8°C, so that on cold
days the inflow is directed through the ground heat storage.

The biomass created by the growth of the microalgae is harvested using an
algae cutter. The energy contained in the biomass can be converted into natural gas through a biological or physical chemical conversion with an efficiency
of about 70–80%. This gaseous fuel can be used in a number of ways (feeding

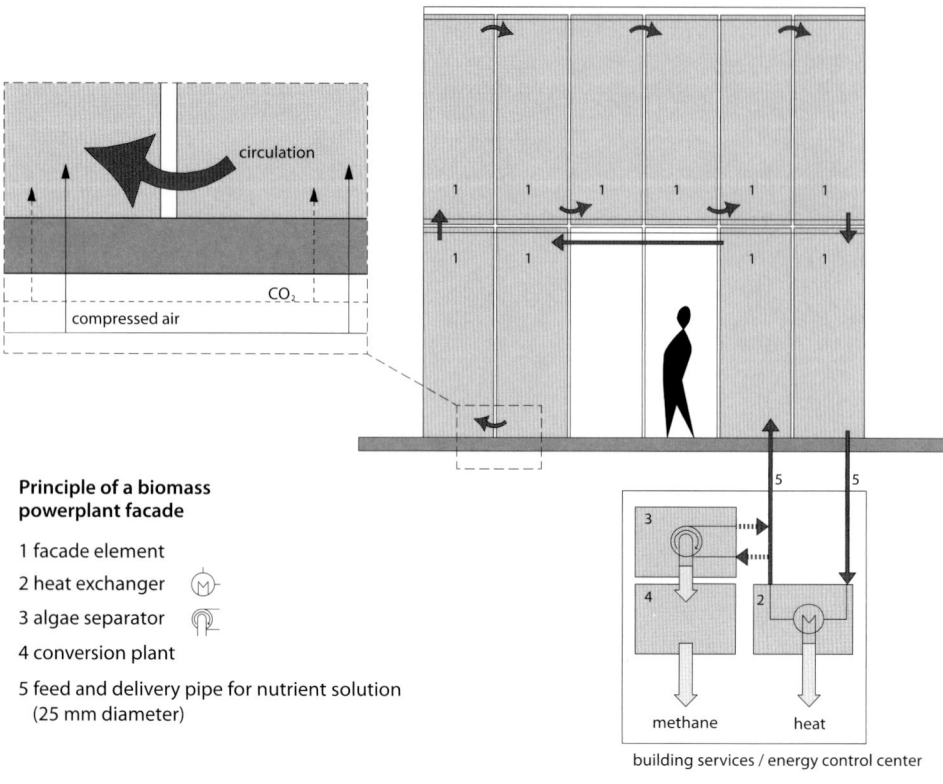

Principle of a biomass powerplant facade

1 facade element
2 heat exchanger
3 algae separator
4 conversion plant
5 feed and delivery pipe for nutrient solution (25 mm diameter)

methane   heat

building services / energy control center

8

8 Diagram showing how the bioreactor facade works. All functions of the bioreactor facade – heat generation, biomass production, and flue gas clearing – are directly coupled with the in-building systems (reproduction: ©Arup GmbH).

into the public natural gas grid, used in the tanks of natural gas-fueled cars, used in communal heating/power stations), and can be stored with almost no loss.

Automated process and plant automation enable the continual cultivation and utilization of the algae at the site of the building, with the minimum of maintenance costs. The necessary additional building systems can be integrated into existing in-building system solutions as a plug-in. The supply and drainage of water for the bioreactors can be provided by the municipal water supply and wastewater system.

Innovation

In 2010, the SPLITTERWERK team won their first award for their involvement in a competition to implement a Smart Material House at the Internationale Bauausstellung (IBA) Hamburg in 2013. An outstanding feature of their design was a bioreactor facade with a surface area of more than 200m², which was drafted in association with Arup, who then created the plan for it. In a research project funded by the German ZukunftBau federal research initiative, the firms Arup, SSC, and COLT are developing a system-based solution for back-ventilated facades constructed from flat-panel photobioreactors positioned on a single axis. Plans for the appropriate facade system have been completed; in January 2012 the first prototypes were installed at a test site in Hamburg. The first evaluations of yield values suggest that the plan is a success. Modifications with the aim of optimizing heat yields are ongoing.

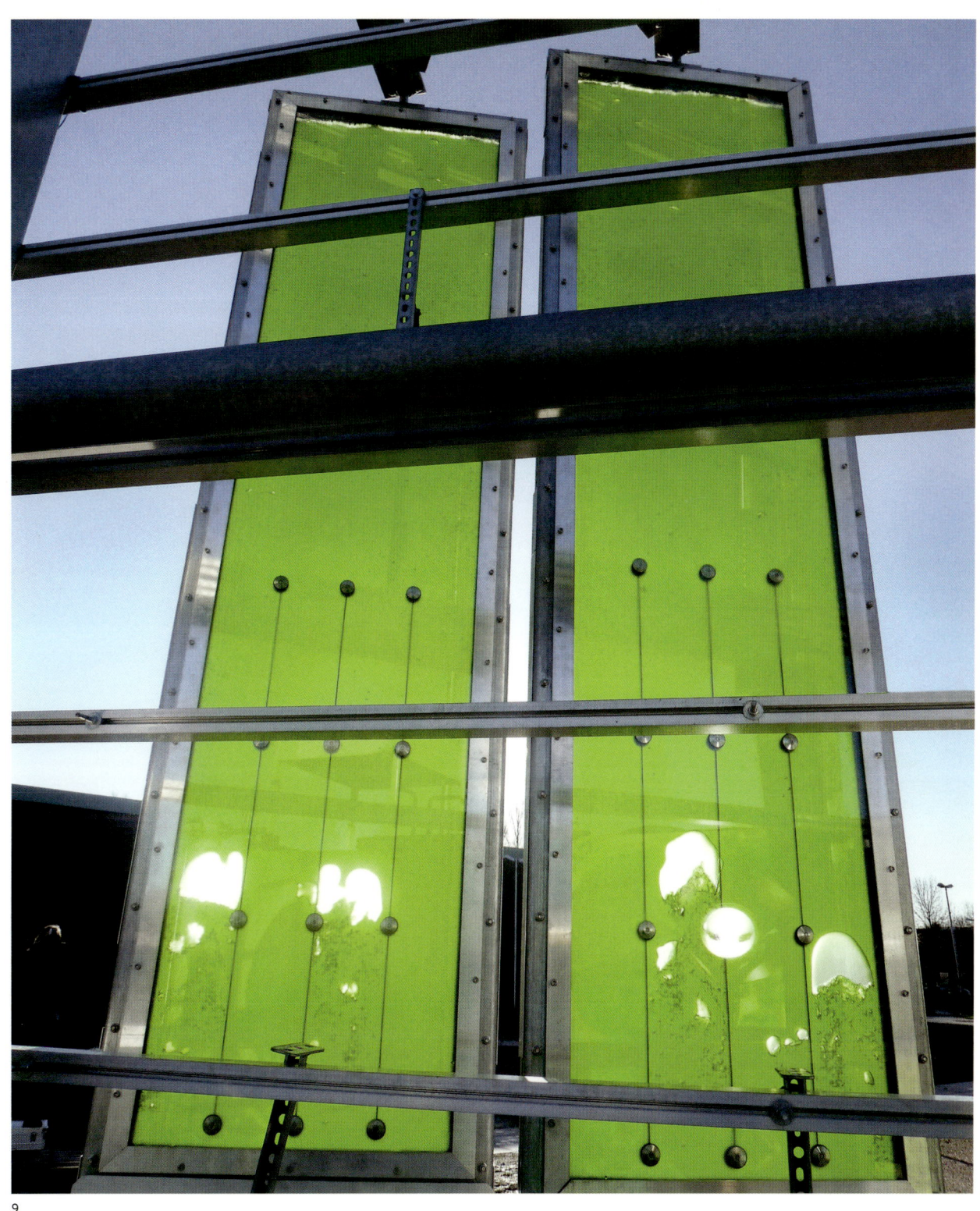

9

9 Rear side of the prototype, on
the test site

10   11

10 Front side of the prototype, on the test site

11 External sun protection slats as a possible application area for PBRs, for regulation of incoming daylight – Project PSD Bank

The photobioreactors are integrated into story-high vertical slats with a width of approximately 70cm. The glazing is constructed in four layers. The reactor space within which the medium circulates is located between the two inner panes. Insulating air-filled cavities are positioned on both sides of the reactor space to reduce heat loss. The outermost layer consists of white antireflective glass on the front and cover glass with free decoration on the back. Further funding will allow this technology to be developed and to establish itself on the market in a similar way to photovoltaic technology.

The next immediate step in the testing phase is to integrate the system into industrial and commercial premises in order to dispose of the CO_2 arising from their process chains. The large surface areas of the facade and roof surfaces of single-level industrial buildings help to make operating such a system economically viable. The bioreactor facade is feasible for retrofitting in existing constructions as well as for new structures. Installing bioreactors can significantly improve the design properties of an existing building. This system could develop into a key technology for CO_2-neutral developments and districts – with the production rate of the algae and therefore the rate of CO_2 removal made visually apparent by the way the facade becomes green. As a further refinement of solar thermal components, PBRs represent an ideal addition to building-integrated PV, especially in the implementation of plus energy buildings. The facade's usefulness consists in producing biomass and heat, thereby improving the energy budget, the reduction of CO_2 emissions, and the regulation of light and radiation penetration. A number of different possible installation situations exist in the roof and the facade, and are currently being simulated and evalu-

12

12 Simulation of the Smart Material House at the IBA 2013 in Hamburg with 200m² of integrated PBRs

ated in current research projects. The first building with a bioreactor facade – known as the "Smart Treefrog" – will be created in 2013, in connection with the Internationale Bauausstellung (IBA) in Hamburg.

Facade Recycling

Linda Hildebrand
Daniel Arztmann

Vision

Effective concepts are required to combat the impact of the climate crisis. Expected demographic developments and their resulting energy consumption call for sensible solutions. Concern for the environment is no longer a peripheral issue. It is now clear in all sectors – including construction – that a serious sustainability strategy and an environmentally friendly image are essential elements in positive publicity. One significant reflection of this is the increased certification of new buildings.

The tasks of the construction sector

The construction sector is responsible for more than half of the raw materials consumed worldwide and over 60% of all waste produced [71], making it a special case. The consequences of these figures are very clear: the construction sector is more in need of change than other industrial sectors, and also has more potential for change. Recyclability of products is recommended as a starting point for improving the situation, as analysis of the intensive consumption of resources during the construction process shows. This is backed up by an innovative ecological product development process, with documentation to show the feasibility of environmentally appropriate implementation.

The construction industry takes raw materials from nature in order to produce heat, cooling, and power. The consumption of this energy in the operation of buildings correlates with operating costs. Lowering consumption is in the inter-

1 Production of
element facades

2 Assembly of
element facades

ests of the operator, and also minimizes impact on the environment. Raw materials and the energy derived from them for use in construction and demolition of a building's structure – "gray energy" – have hitherto received less attention. As operating energy consumption declines, however, this value is becoming increasingly relevant. For a building that complies with the 2007 German Energy Savings Ordinance (EnEV), for instance, gray energy levels are equal to operating energy levels over a period of thirty years.

Gray energy levels can be calculated and evaluated using life cycle assessment. This involves listing and evaluating all raw materials required for the production process, together with all harmful emissions. Nonrenewable primary energy and global warming potential are the most commonly used indicators. This overview of energy use must take account both of the operation energy and of gray energy.

Balancing environmental impact against quality makes particular requirements of the architect. More than was previously the case, architects must examine the consumption of materials and energy and justify it in terms of quality delivered. Aside from the economic issues, the incorporation of ecological aspects increases the need for decisions to be well considered and, subsequently, clearly presented. Architects and planners have to give more thought to whether investment of energy will be justified by an increase in quality.

3

4

5

3 Inclusion of silicon in molten glass

4 Contamination of glass by PVB film

5 Compound materials for insulation walls

Methods

Three strategies exist for optimizing the environmental impact of buildings:

> improving the cost-benefit ratio (increased efficiency);
> saving energy and reducing the associated emissions (sufficiency);
> restructuring to accommodate new energy forms (new energy structures).

Increased efficiency

Efficiency denotes the achieving of a goal with a minimum of effort. In this context, it means deriving maximum quality from a minimum of raw materials while minimizing CO_2 emissions. Transparent presentation of energy use is an important indicator for the efficient operation of a building in Germany. The German Energy Savings Ordinance (EnEV) requires building owners to produce the figures for their properties.

Sufficiency

The simplest way of reducing cost and carbon dioxide emissions is to restrict consumption. Intelligent use of energy is one way of avoiding excessive consumption of energy for heating. Passive measures are of particular significance to the construction sector. The avoidance of ventilation and transmission heat loss via the facade has a significant impact on the amount of energy needed for heating and cooling. Construction standards have risen since the oil crisis of the

6

7

6 Waste from facade
production

7 Scrap category:
aluminium cuts

1970s, and look set to conform to European demands for "nearly zero-energy building" standards over the next few years.

New energy structures

Renewable energy provides light and heat and releases less CO_2, as it does not use fossil fuels and therefore produces no fossil fuel emissions. As of 2012, a resolution to increase the level of renewable energy use from 5.8% (the 2006 level) to 20% by 2020 has been enshrined in law [72]. It is the intention of legislators that requiring grid operators being to buy power from renewable energy systems at a fixed price will act as an incentive for adoption.

Increased efficiency for facades

Innovative ways of changing how we make use of diminishing resources while contributing to reducing emissions can be realized by means of specific planning strategies within the building industry. In this case, standard practice in the recycling of facades was the example taken as the object of study.

Specifically, the recycling potential of an element facade was investigated [73]. Element facades' extensive prefabrication makes them a likely choice for use in large-scale projects involving full glazing. We can assume that after their projected useful life of fifty years, a large proportion of facades of this type will enter the recycling process.

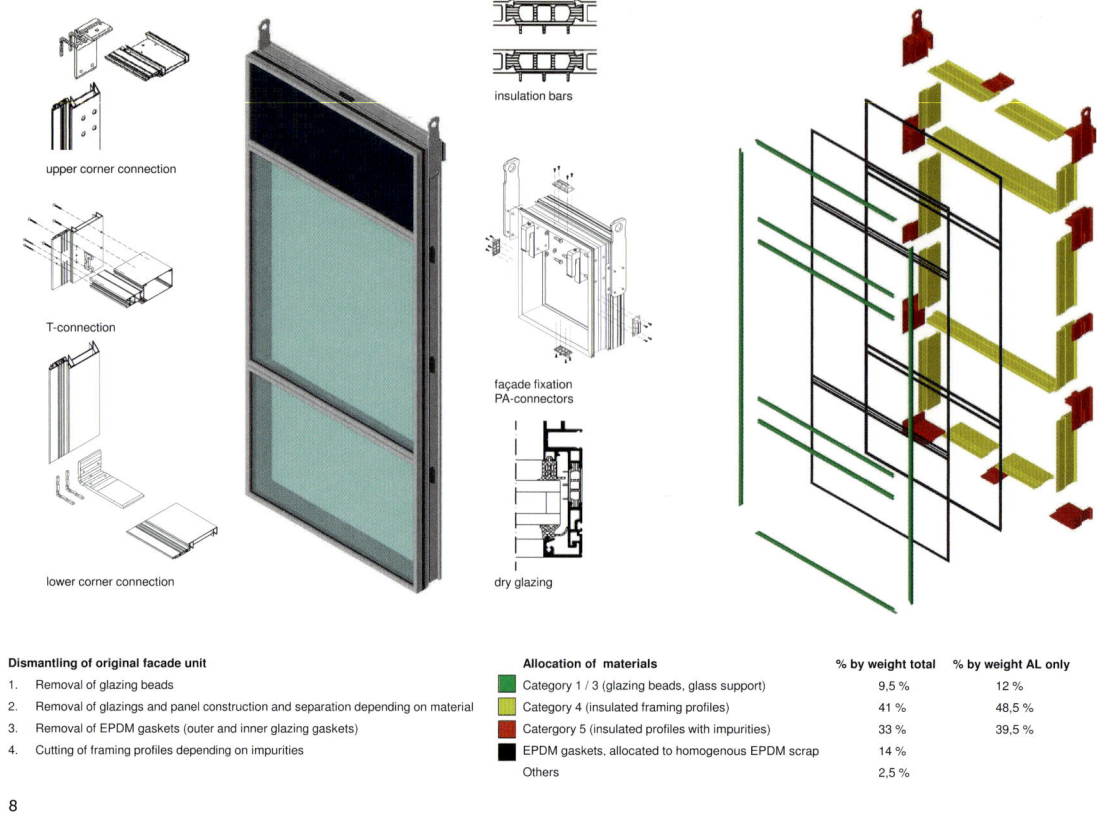

upper corner connection

T-connection

lower corner connection

insulation bars

façade fixation
PA-connectors

dry glazing

Dismantling of original facade unit
1. Removal of glazing beads
2. Removal of glazings and panel construction and separation depending on material
3. Removal of EPDM gaskets (outer and inner glazing gaskets)
4. Cutting of framing profiles depending on impurities

Allocation of materials	% by weight total	% by weight AL only
Category 1 / 3 (glazing beads, glass support)	9,5 %	12 %
Category 4 (insulated framing profiles)	41 %	48,5 %
Catergory 5 (insulated profiles with impurities)	33 %	39,5 %
EPDM gaskets, allocated to homogenous EPDM scrap	14 %	
Others	2,5 %	

8

8 Recycling plan for original facade

The analysis of the facade system's recycling properties began with an investigation of the materials used and the ways in which they are connected and combined. The principal material is aluminum, which is used for the facade profiles and numerous additional components. In addition, several types of plastic, such as EPDM, polyamide, polyethylene and PVC, are used in large amounts, with the addition of small amounts of stainless steel. By themselves, almost all of these materials possess extremely favorable recycling properties – especially aluminum, which is almost 100% recyclable. In order to exploit this potential for recycling fully, however, it is necessary to separate the materials completely. The way in which the materials are combined and whether the combinations can be dissolved is the significant factor. The spectrum ranges from easily dissolvable connections, in which the materials can be separated out without deterioration or contamination with detrimental substances, to combinations that are irreversible or reversible only to a limited extent. The plastics compounds that are in frequent use represent a particular challenge; to create them, two or more plastics are "blended" together at the production stage in such a way that separating them out at a later stage is either impossible or economically unfeasible.

Materials analysis has shown that, for element facades in current use, major expenditure of resources is required to separate out the constituent materials. This prevents the recycling potential of their components from being fully exploited. In addition, the individual constituents of the facade are not labeled, making it difficult to distinguish between materials with a similar appearance. As a consequence, only materials that can readily be isolated and separated out

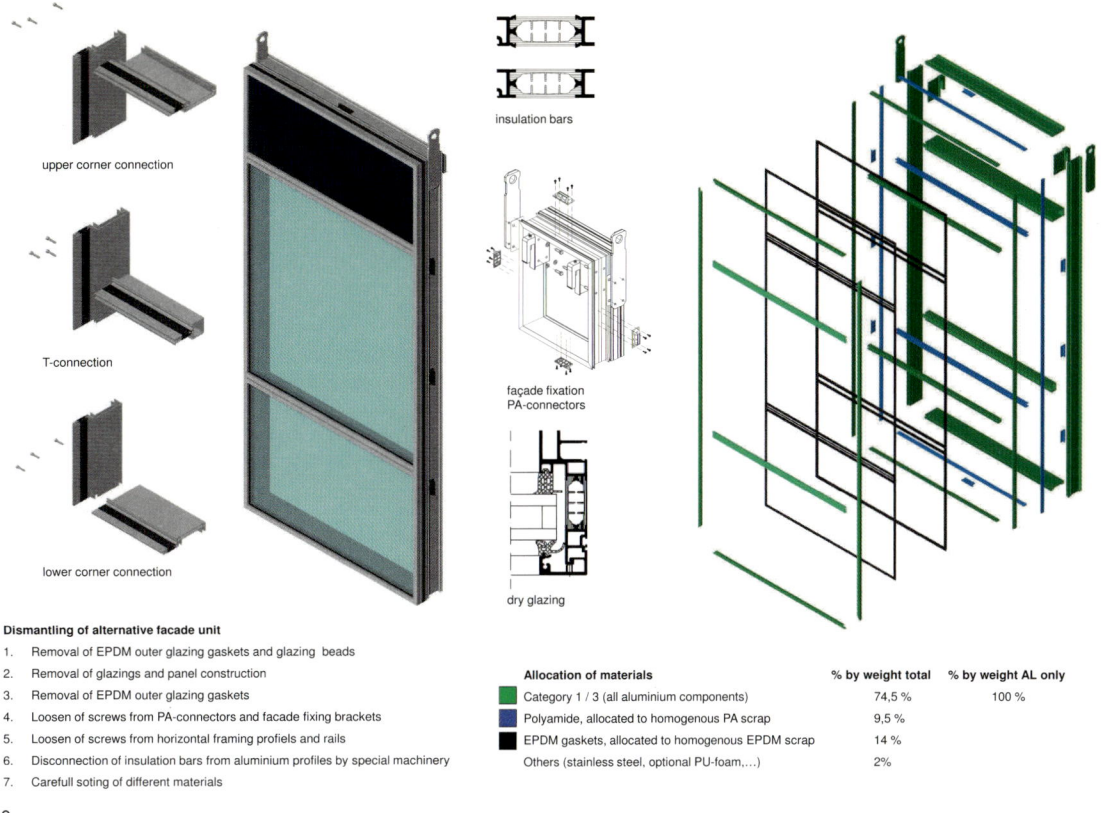

upper corner connection

T-connection

lower corner connection

insulation bars

façade fixation
PA-connectors

dry glazing

Dismantling of alternative facade unit

1. Removal of EPDM outer glazing gaskets and glazing beads
2. Removal of glazings and panel construction
3. Removal of EPDM outer glazing gaskets
4. Loosen of screws from PA-connectors and facade fixing brackets
5. Loosen of screws from horizontal framing profiels and rails
6. Disconnection of insulation bars from aluminium profiles by special machinery
7. Carefull soting of different materials

9

Allocation of materials	% by weight total	% by weight AL only
■ Category 1 / 3 (all aluminium components)	74,5 %	100 %
■ Polyamide, allocated to homogenous PA scrap	9,5 %	
■ EPDM gaskets, allocated to homogenous EPDM scrap	14 %	
Others (stainless steel, optional PU-foam,…)	2%	

9 Recycling plan for alternative facade

can actually be recycled. The remainder of the facade construction is broken down and sorted into various grades of scrap, depending on the levels of contaminants. At the next stage, these waste materials may be downcycled into inferior products, reused as raw materials, thermally utilized, or disposed of.

Innovation

The master's thesis "Recycling von Fassadesystemen" ("Recycling of facade systems") contributed to the evaluation of the potential for improving the recycling options for this kind of facade by proposing the development of an alternative facade type that would allow ways of solving the above-mentioned problems to be found and implemented [73]. The starting points for this investigation were:

> the number of different materials used;
> the ease with which the materials can be identified;
> the subsequent feasibility of separating the construction complex for recycling.

Optimization produced a reduction in the number of plastics used: whereas seven types of plastic were found to be present in the original facade construction, the alternative facade plan reduced the number to three. These three types of plastic could easily be distinguished from each other due to their different degrees of hardness. Reversible connections were integrated into the facade construction with minimal expenditure, making it easier to dismantle the facade components. The alternative facade also dispensed with the use of compound materials.

Comparing the original facade construction with the alternative facade reveals that the recycling qualities of technical products can be improved – dramatically, in some cases – by simple means. The amount of aluminum contained in the original facade construction that could be reused without quality deterioration was approximately 12%. Simple changes to the connections between the components in the alternative facade allow this percentage to be increased by almost 100%.

The recycling qualities of a technical product, however, do not depend solely on recycling-oriented product development. Clear communication of recycling properties – so that the recycling operator is aware of all the adaptations that have been made – is equally important. A recycling passport of the type described by VDI Directive 2243 [74] appears to be indicated. The recycling passport should contain "all information relevant to recycling together with a perspective view image of the product, a list of the materials it contains and their respective weights, the names of the substances that must be extracted and treated separately (e.g. contaminants), and any potentially damaging substances and components, indications of how to remove these substances and of reusable materials and components and a tabular list giving all substance groups contained in the products."

These specifications were taken as the basis for the sample recycling passports for the facade systems described above. A recycling passport of this kind must be available to recycling providers at the right time and in the right place; given the projected lifespan of an element facade – about fifty years – this represents a challenge. Radio-frequency identification (RFID) might offer one possible solution to this problem. This involves storing all the relevant information pertaining to the construction components used on a chip. The chip is secured to the facade element, allowing the information to be retrieved using an RFID reader so that the materials can be recirculated.

Future Prospects

Regardless of whether or not human activity is responsible for global warming, its proven impact on the environment creates a need to act. The current debate has led to calls for the restructuring of consumer behavior to recognize environmental concerns as well as economic concerns and, ideally, to combine them. The more sustainable reuse of construction products described here is one possible way forward for the industry in meeting these demands. It is important to make responsible use of the available materials in such a way that subsequent generations are not disadvantaged.

It can be stated that schemes to improve recycling properties significantly depend on three factors:

> factor 1: taking into account recycling properties during product development, primarily in the selection of materials and in the way they are combined;
> factor 2: communication of recycling options to the recycling provider, so that the materials can be thoroughly and correctly separated. This can be ensured by means of intelligent construction and through clear identification of the products;
> factor 3: in the final stage, it is important that the retrieved raw materials really can be reused at the same quality level, as this is the best way of ensuring the reuse of our world's natural resources without loss of quality.

Further measures are needed to bring these specific insights together in a wider context. The example shown here sufficiently demonstrates the results of responsible planning and construction product use. It identifies a new strategy for taking a construction concept for construction products and (certified) buildings and arriving at a demonstrably "green" product by means of innovative resource management.

It is clear that the balance of energy investment (as an indicator for environmental impact) against quality achieved is a complex area for architects and planners. Building certification schemes, such as the German Sustainable Building Certificate (DGNB), create transparency for customers and the responsibility of proof for planners. It is they who must reconcile the demands of ecology, the economy and society in order to meet the responsibility of optimizing the environmental impact of the construction sector by creating sustainable buildings.

Within the construction sector, improvements can be made by optimizing products through a multiperspectival product development process. The current perspective on the development of features such as window and facade systems is excessively biased toward improving individual factors, such as component-specific heat-permeability coefficients. Legislation in the various countries is now so exacting that these values can be achieved only by using application-specific materials or compound materials. The manufacture of these materials is extremely energy-intensive, and, as mentioned above, their disposal is extremely problematic. On the other hand, the past few years have seen the materials consumption and environmental impact of the construction industry decline to such an extent that an assessment of the gray energy expended on the materials locked up in construction components can no longer be ignored.

Wohn-Vision-2020

Recycling Design for the Living Spaces of the Future

Verena Wriedt
Mark Fleischhauer

Vision

The aim of the Wohn-Vision-2020 research project was to help strengthen the position of small to medium-sized companies (SMEs), and to provide opportunities for disadvantaged young people and long-term unemployed people by developing forward-looking visions for interior furnishing that make good use of resources. The intention behind this project, which was sponsored by the Deutsche Bundesstiftung Umwelt (DBU), was to create an innovative network in which different agencies' requirements and competencies would complement one another, in order to create a win-win situation for the various partners from the fields of design, education, production, advertising, and sales. It culminated in an exhibition of 1:1 scale representations of visions for furniture made from used materials – intended for living spaces, workspaces, leisure spaces, bathing spaces, rest spaces, and cooking and communicating spaces – held in July 2011 [66].

People are increasingly looking for home-design concepts that are flexible enough to permit adaptation to changed lifestyle requirements. The overriding thought behind this is that every person should be able to live in his or her familiar surroundings (house, apartment, or room) for as long as possible. The expert view is that no society (growing, stagnant, or shrinking) can afford to ignore its population's increasing need for home-design concepts with new qualities and values [67]. These thoughts led to the drafting of the following parameters for designing future interior furnishing visions in the Wohn-Vision-2020 project:

1

1 Wohn-Vision-2020 started in May 2009 and ended with a final exhibition in the foyer of the Detmold School of Architecture and Interior Design, Hochschule Ostwestfalen Lippe

> Recycling as a basic principle: the utilization of used materials to improve resource efficiency
> Barrier-free living spaces: guaranteed socioeconomic participation for all, regardless of factors such as disability, gender, age, and level of education
> Flexible floor plans: adaptation to life's changing requirements
> Minimizing climate change and adaptation: reduction of greenhouse gas emissions and adaptation to the inevitable consequences of climate change.

In particular, the Wohn-Vision-2020 project concentrated on deploying used materials. In workshops, design experts and students established that in implementing the project, particular emphasis should be placed on previously unexploited mechanical, aesthetic, and atmospheric properties [68].

The production processes upon which the project was founded were designed to provide disadvantaged young people and long-term unemployed people with useful skills. The intention was that the manufacturing process for the interior furnishing designs would principally require manual skills, discernment, patience, and creativity – important prerequisites for a successful qualification. In addition, the following criteria specifically relating to materials were defined:

1. Dismantling: Products intended for use can be isolated – by disassembly, melting down, or cutting, for instance – in such a way that the materials obtained do not become waste.

2a

2b

2c

3a

3b

3c

2 MyTie by Celia Günther

3a,b Piet and Pepe by
Nina Kreitsmann, renderings

3c Piet and Pepe by
Nina Kreitsmann, prototype

2. Designing series: Postconsumer materials and secondary raw materials are used to create new product series, e.g., cushions made from ties or broad couches made from pallet wood.
3. Ready-mades: The usability of selected furniture or components is altered or expanded by combining two or more elements.

Method

These basic conditions and principles served as guidelines for the ten different partners (see below), who were integrated into the multistage process according to their different types of know-how relating to design, education, manufacture, advertising, and distribution. The project comprised the following phases:

> Development and representation of future living spaces
> Design and assembly of prototypes made from used materials
> Taking prototypes forward to serial production
> Sale of the furniture

Recycling design communication campaigns – such as the recycling design prize awarded by the RecyclingBörse! Herford since 2007 – were run to coincide with the project.

4

4a

4b

4 kommod and kommod2sit by
Jana Niggemeier, rendering

4a,b kommod by
Jana Niggemeier, prototype

Results

Responding to the demands of future living spaces

One of the most important results was that the concepts that were developed contributed to meeting anticipated changes relating to future living conditions and functions:

> the living room and the kitchen merge to form a space for activities with family and friends
> the bedroom and the bathroom merge to form an oasis for relaxation
> a multifunctional space takes on the roles of workspace, music room, home cinema etc.
> to create a living space in which children can grow up and adults can grow old, flexibility is required

The students designed furniture based on the future scenarios developed in the first phase of the Wohn-Vision-2020 project, to accommodate increasing requirements in terms of mobility, flexibility, communication, withdrawal, and relaxation:

> Flexibility: MyTie by Celia Günther can be adjusted to serve either as a sofa or a divan bed.
> Variability: the Piet and Pepe designs by Nina Kreitsmann can be used as bar stools, armchairs, trestles, bowls, or tables.

5a

5b

5a Kentrum kitchen table by
Maria Schewzow, prototype

5b Kentrum kitchen table by
Maria Schewzow, detail

6 fiet by Belinda Bergener,
rendering

6a,b,c fiet by Belinda Bergener,
prototype

> Adaptability: kommod and kommod2sit by Jana Niggemeier are inter-
changeable in terms of both style and use.
> Foldability: fiet by Belinda Bergener can be converted from minimal mate-
rial thickness for transportation to large-scale shelves or seating elements
in a single stage. The Kentrum kitchen table by Maria Schewzow can be
extended by deploying a folding leaf.
> Divisibility: Julia Ebbeskotte's space divider permits division into personal
and public zones.

Contribution to sustainability

In addition to conserving materials, the project contributes to sustainability in
many other areas:

Field	Details
Ecological	reducing waste by using old materials for furniture production reducing greenhouse gas emissions reducing water consumption reducing air pollution
Economic	increased employment (provided by a number of manufacturers) through new and growing market segments, each with its own consumer group new product types to increase profits for designers and retailers
Social	Labor-intensive production: workplace niches for people with disabilities and skills-development schemes
Cultural	Recycling design products encourage environmental debate and can potentially promote behavioral change and the replacement of a throwaway culture with a culture of recycling. The project may also stimulate the everyday creativity of individuals.

6

6a

6b

6c

Positive environmental impact and resource efficiency in a life cycle concept

Life cycle phase	Details
Extraction and processing of resources	Resources from bulk refuse or clearances are collected on a local, or, at most, a regional level. Most of the material is processed manually, often in workshops for people with disabilities.
Design	Product design is based around secondary raw materials (mostly particle board). Every new piece of furniture consists of 80–90% used materials, which are checked for the presence of formaldehyde and other harmful substances. As one of the project's design principles, materials without harmful substances are given a label [69].
Manufacture and retail	Products are primarily made by hand or using small-scale machines. Most manufacturers are also outlets, ensuring low or zero production-site-to-sales-outlet transport costs.
Distribution	The distribution of the furniture covers a wider area than resource extraction, with around 75% of the furniture being sold up to 300km from the manufacturing site.
Use	The distinctive character of the new furniture designs, together with a certain degree of identification with the product (customer's requests are often taken into account during manufacture) result in the furniture remaining in use for a longer period on average.
Collectors	The process of collecting old recycled furniture does not differ significantly from the collection of conventional furnishings.
Reuse, recycling, energy, restoration, disposal	There is no significant difference from conventional furniture in this respect either.

7

7a

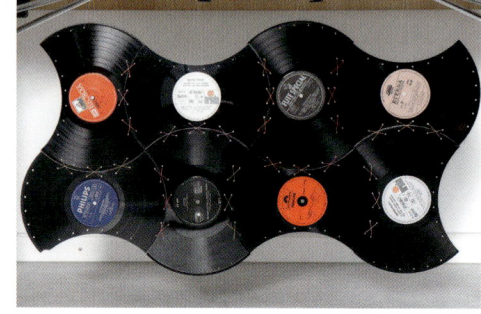

7b

7c

7 room partitions by
Julia Ebbeskotte, rendering

7a,b room partitions by
Julia Ebbeskotte, prototype

7c room partitions by
Julia Ebbeskotte, prototype
lamp shade.

The basic thought behind the production of furniture from used materials was to extend the useful life of these materials. However, there are other aspects – such as the quality of the design – that can extend a product's period of use. Qualitative product life cycle assessments were drawn up relating to these aspects:

Fig. 8 gives a picture of the potential resource savings in terms of relative values and initial qualitative assessments, taking electricity use as an example. The flowcharts show conventional furniture production on the one hand and recycled furniture production on the other. The comparison shows that significant improvements can be achieved in terms of the ecological balance sheet, as the energy consumed in recycling furniture production is about 63% lower than for conventional furniture production [70].

Due to the unavailability of data, only reasonable assumptions can be formulated for the standard environmental indicators. By analogy with energy consumption, reductions of between 50% and 75% have been projected for other environmentally significant factors.

Innovation

The Wohn-Vision-2020 is innovative in the following respects:

> Product: new products made from new materials with a unique design
> Procedures: slow production by including underprivileged social groups

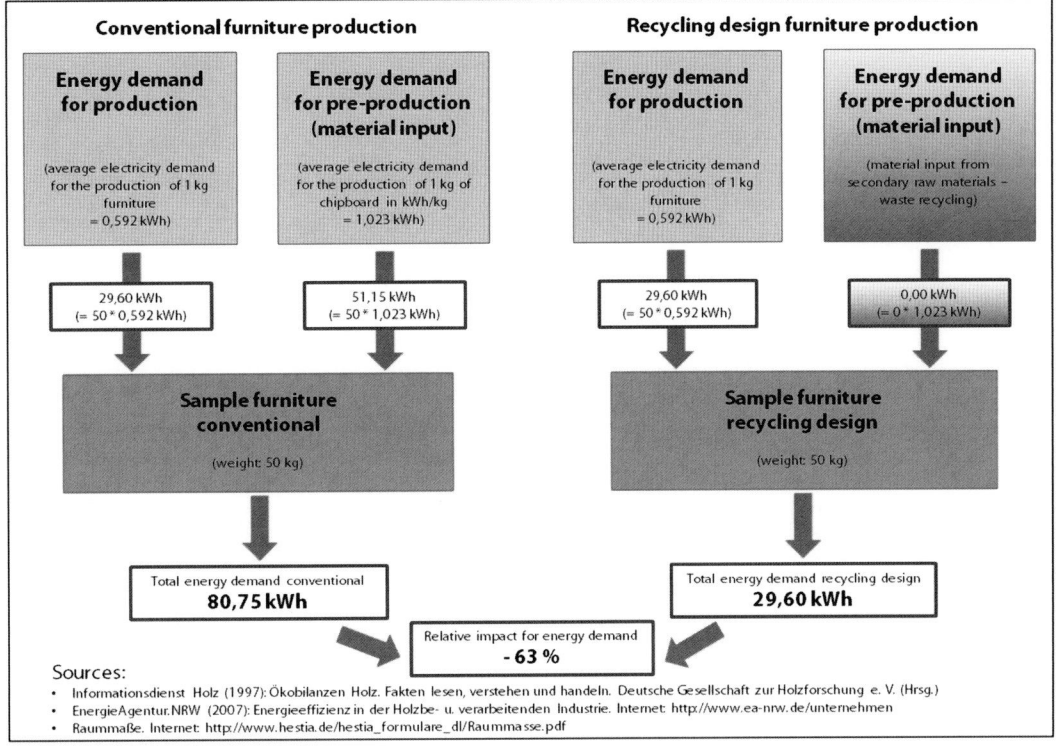

Improvement of environmental performance: Relative impact for energy demand

Conventional furniture production

Energy demand for production
(average electricity demand for the production of 1 kg furniture = 0,592 kWh)

Energy demand for pre-production (material input)
(average electricity demand for the production of 1 kg of chipboard in kWh/kg = 1,023 kWh)

29,60 kWh (= 50 * 0,592 kWh)

51,15 kWh (= 50 * 1,023 kWh)

Sample furniture conventional

(weight: 50 kg)

Total energy demand conventional **80,75 kWh**

Relative impact for energy demand **- 63 %**

Recycling design furniture production

Energy demand for production
(average electricity demand for the production of 1 kg furniture = 0,592 kWh)

Energy demand for pre-production (material input)
(material input from secondary raw materials – waste recycling)

29,60 kWh (= 50 * 0,592 kWh)

0,00 kWh (= 0 * 1,023 kWh)

Sample furniture recycling design

(weight: 50 kg)

Total energy demand recycling design **29,60 kWh**

Sources:
- Informationsdienst Holz (1997): Ökobilanzen Holz. Fakten lesen, verstehen und handeln. Deutsche Gesellschaft zur Holzforschung e. V. (Hrsg.)
- EnergieAgentur.NRW (2007): Energieeffizienz in der Holzbe- u. verarbeitenden Industrie. Internet: http://www.ea-nrw.de/unternehmen
- Raummaße. Internet: http://www.hestia.de/hestia_formulare_dl/Raummasse.pdf

8

8 Example of reduction of environmental impact in absolute terms

> Technology: development of new production techniques, as used materials require new approaches
> Processes: the development of entirely new ideas for organization and interconnection
> Layout: the development of furniture that is flexible in its applications and operation

The impact of these innovations must be judged in an economic context. They are best expressed in the specific constitution of the production factors that contribute to more sustainable products and production processes. The aim of the environmental protection strategy adopted by the Wohn-Vision-2020 project – and of the furniture ideas listed above – was to combine production factors in an innovative process so as to optimize existing potential and exploit any possible synergies. Expressed in terms of production factors as understood in classic economic theory, the implementation of the environmental protection strategy takes the following form:

> Land and natural resources: sparing use of raw materials (ecological value)
> Work: work-intensive production that requires manual skills, discernment, patience, and creativity, and enables people with disabilities and to disadvantaged sections of the population to acquire valuable skills (social value)
> Capital: cost-efficient production and resources (economic value)
> Human/intellectual/social capital: close ties between design, production, and sale (creative value)

Optimizing

Planning Tools

Measuring Light – Calculating Geometry

José Miguel Martínez Rico
Sergio Saiz Bombín
Aitor Leceta Murguzur

Vision

Building envelope and architecture

The main developments in contemporary architecture focus on the building envelope. We emphasize two distinct conditions that govern its materialisation: a search for continuity in the skin and a better control of energy flow through the envelope.

Hans Ibelings described the status of architectural trends at the end of the twentieth century: "Abstraction arises in radical contrast to the extravagance and deconstructivist complexity that have constituted the aesthetic frame of reference for the past two decades. This simplicity is not primarily a reaction to the aesthetic of visual excess, although that aspect certainly plays a role. In essence the new abstraction is an expression of a fundamentally different attitude to architecture, which it sees less and less as significant and filled with symbolic meaning, and more and more as a neutral object [75]."

The New Museum of Contemporary Art in New York clearly illustrates this idea. Designed as a set of boxes placed on top of one another, the off-center arrangement of the boxes generates a dynamic but self-controlled effect. The continuous skin is sparingly marked with windows, offering views of the city, but does not blight the clear, ardent and abstract image of the building. The skin is made of a silver-plated aluminum expanded metal mesh, which is able to respond to changes in artificial and natural light, to generate varying ambiances within the building.

1

High-tech or supermodern architecture must now take a more sustainable path in construction, above any stylistic considerations. Neutral and efficient facades can significantly enhance the sustainability credentials of a building, and improve energy efficiency by regulating the flow of energy through the envelope and avoiding seasonal fluctuations in temperature.

Much of the research in facade design is now focusing on thermal and solar transmittance. We need simple design tools to quantify the performance of systems for practical, logical, and widespread application.

Method

Metal screens and solar factor

There are a range of solutions that meet the requirements for a neutral and efficient facade. We can define these as *metallic translucent facades*, which are finished with woven metal fabrics, perforated metal sheets, or expanded metal meshes. Their translucency acts as a solar control layer and permits visual contact between inside and outside through the envelope. Placing them outside the glazed and opaque parts of the skin homogenizes the exterior image of the building as it blurs the difference between hollow and solid. This research is focused on the performance of expanded metal meshes as solar control devices.

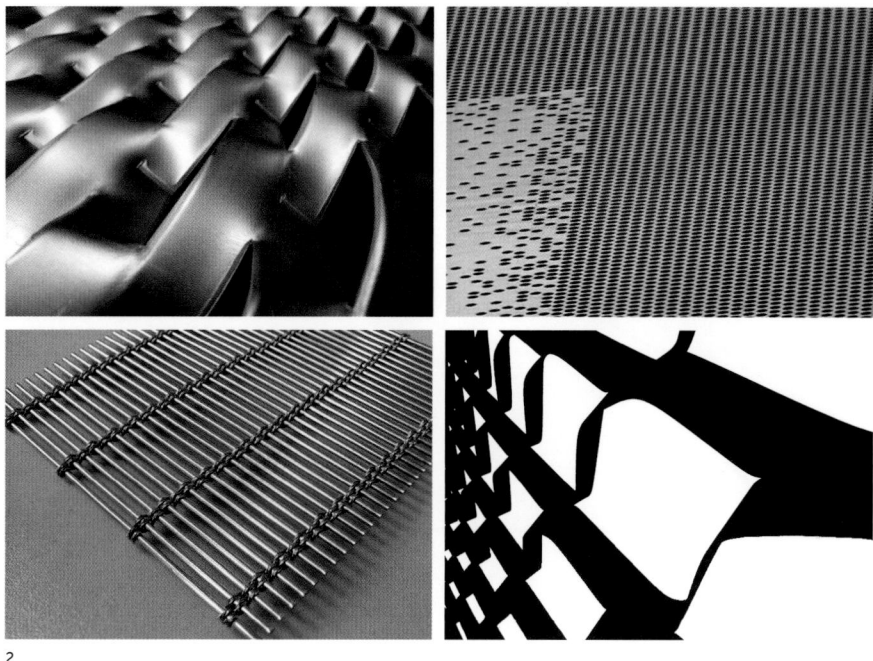

2

2 Different types of metal
screens

The solar factor is between 0 and 1 and indicates the percentage of solar radiation or thermal energy entering a window, glazed element, or solar control device. Another useful value is the daylight factor; this refers only to light and not thermal energy. The expanded metal meshes' ability to absorb and re-emit radiation depends on the color and type of material, its shape, and ventilation of the envelope.

Tools for assessment

The geometry of expanded metal meshes induces a complex behavior of radiation. Reflection, absorption, and radiation are important considerations, when analyzing the solar and luminous character of expanded metals. There are three methods of analysis:

> Computer simulation
> Laboratory simulation
> Analysis of real solar radiation

The objective is to quantify solar and luminous transmittance and reflectance. The angle at which the solar or light beam hits the metal (the angle of incidence) dictates the transmittance capabilities of the metal.

Testing several samples will highlight the parameters affecting the performance of an expanded metal sheet as a solar control device, and which combinations of parameters provide an accurate relationship between solar and luminous transmittance.

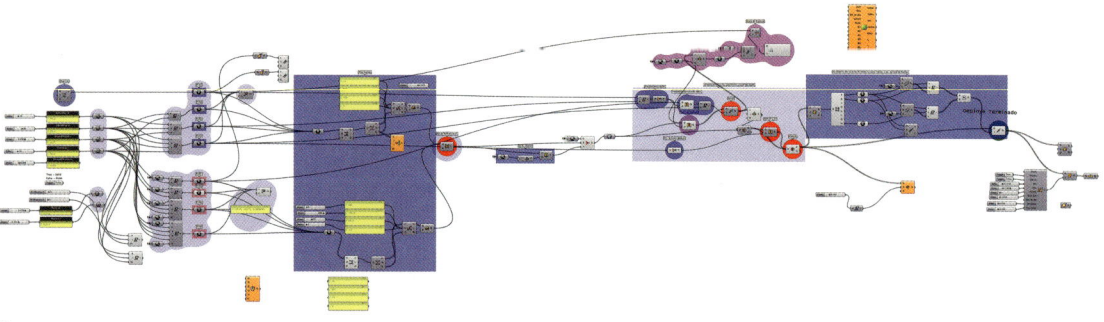

3

4

5

3 Visual representation of
a parametric control of the
geometry of expanded metal
meshes with the software
Grasshopper

4, 5 Digital simulation of
different lighting situations
through a metal mesh

Results

Computer simulation

A geometrical analysis of the manufacturing process enables the use of parametric design modeling. The parametric design software enables us to create 3D models of the expanded metal meshes. Existing radiation simulation programs can then be used on the 3D models.

These models can be used to obtain the required type of expanded metal mesh for the designer. The shape of the expanded metal depends on several geometrical parameters. There are many possible combinations of these parameters, and consequently a great variety of the geometrical possibilities of expanded metal meshes.

Geometry as a result of the manufacturing process

Expanded metals are simple to manufacture. The process consists of metal coils subjected to shearing and expanding operations in press machines. The resulting mesh is then galvanized or lacquered. The process consists of consecutive cutting and bending operations in discontinuous segments of straight lines [76].

There are several types of expanded metals, each depending on the form of the blade and the shape of the hole. The simplest and most common type has rhom-

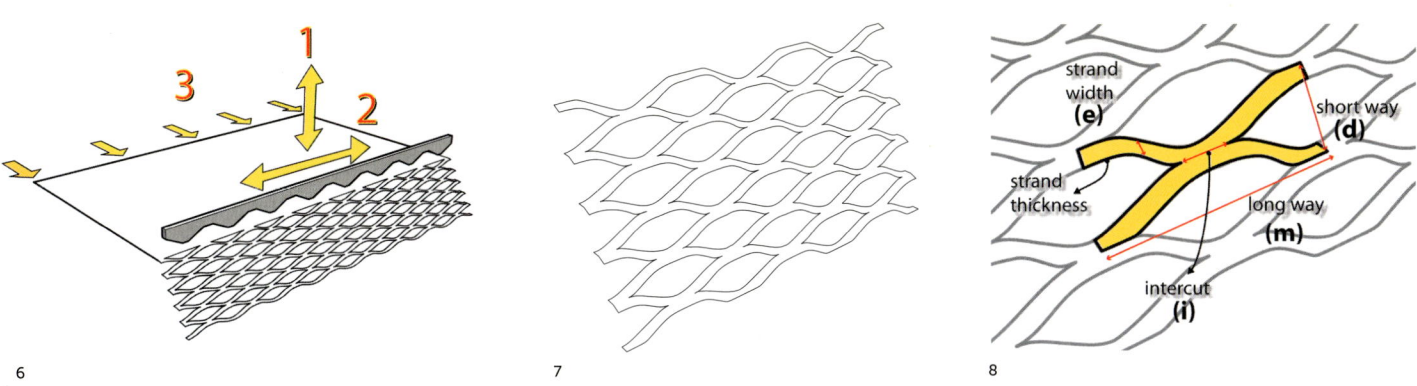

6

7

8

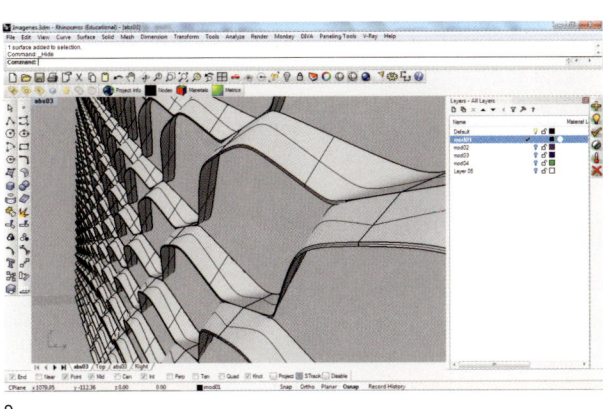

9

6–8 Determining factor of
the geometry of expanded
metal meshes

9 Screenshot of
parametrically designed
model

boid holes. Meshes with hexagonal holes are also a common form. This emu-
lates the circular pattern of perforated sheets but with a significant cost advantage. It produces a different relationship between cross-vision through the mesh
and solar control performance when compared with rhomboid-holed sheets.

Other than solar screen applications, expanded metal sheets have been used in
industrial elements as filters. These meshes can be pressed, formed, and welded
into components for straining, retention, and filtration. They also serve as anti-
slip surfaces for catwalks and ramps, and as reinforcement for walls, mortar, and
plaster works.

When designing a facade the choice of building shape is dictated by the plastic
considerations. In general, we can state that the use of wider strands will obtain
greater reflection of solar radiation. Solutions comprising thinner nerves provide better cross-vision but less sun protection.

Parametric modeling of expanded metal

Parametric modeling allows us to define an object by means of parameters
instead of drawing it directly. We define the attributes of each part of the model
and the relationships between parts or between parts and the environment.

As the objective is to analyze the performance of numerous expanded metal
models, a parametric definition of expanded metal becomes particularly useful.
The Rhinoceros modeling application and its extension Grasshopper were used
to provide the definitions regarding parametric design.

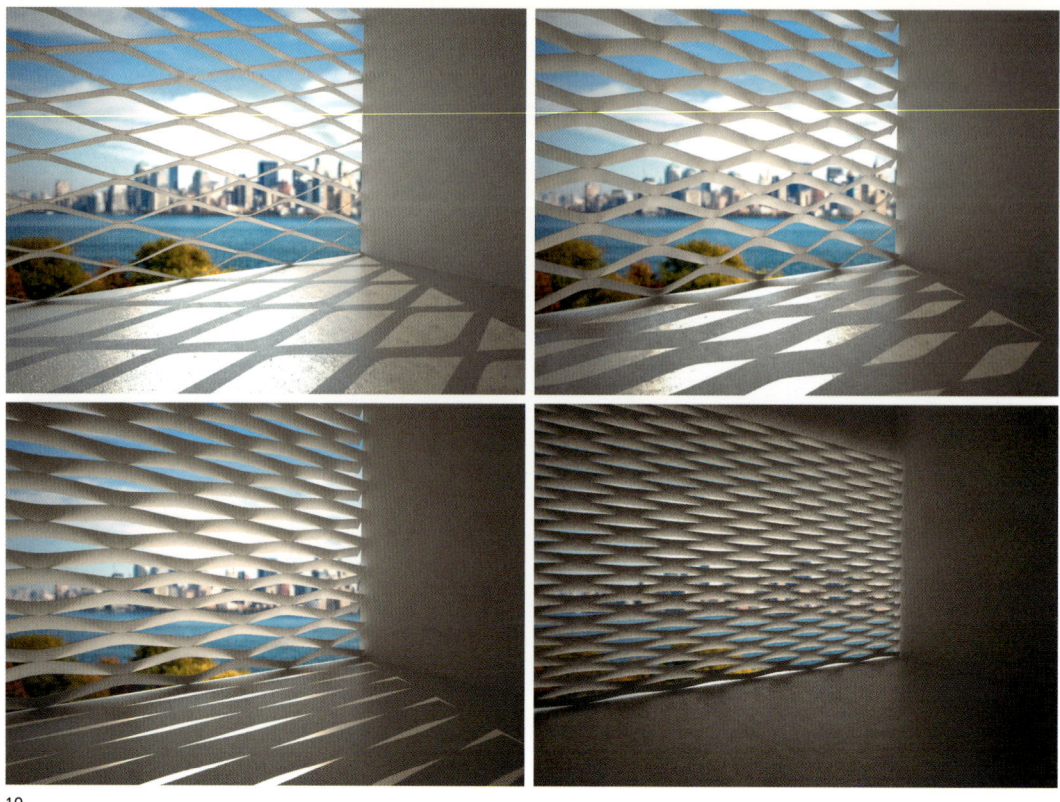

10

10, 11 Different meshes
under identical lighting
conditions

Daylight and thermal computer simulation

The models are exported to the radiation simulation program, which can calculate the daylight factor for a three-dimensional device in a given location and with the device in a given position.

Thermal solar energy behavior is difficult to predict. Considerations must be made regarding the energy absorbed and re-emitted by the device and the heat relief due to ventilation in the gap between the device and the next facade layer.

Laboratory simulations and field tests

Laboratory simulations have two main constituents: the lamp and the sample holder. A rotary sample holder allows us to check several directions of radiation for the fixed lamp. The solar factor of glass is usually measured by precision radiometers, which are designed for small samples.

Field tests on a clear sunny day are most suitable for testing the solar factor of a solar control device. Constant changes in the position of the sun, clearness of the sky, and air movement will produce changes in the amount of radiation and the temperature on-site. The results obtained are then compared with the results from other methods.

11

Innovation

Existing methods for calculating solar paths or trajectories allow us to calculate the angles of incidence that the sun would have in a specific location and at a specific facade orientation. From the results of each test, we can calculate the average solar factor for a specified mesh, geographical situation, and inclination, which can then be used to obtain the thermal and daylight performance of facades with expanded metal meshes.

Following on from this research, a software program will be developed to generate the 3D model of expanded metal mesh and calculate the solar and daylight factor of the device, from specified geometrical parameters, and the position of a facade.

The development of innovative products initially focused on developing new materials and new transformation processes. In some cases, a more efficient design can be achieved by researching into possible improvements of an existing product. This is the case for expanded metal, a metal product invented long ago, which has been widely introduced into the construction field without precise characterization. Obtaining the solar factor values for an expanded metal mesh will improve the thermal efficiency of buildings; it will expand its range of implications and lead to the design of devices with enhanced responsive capabilities and thus facades will be able to adapt to varying solar characteristics.

Digital Design and Construction

Marco Hemmerling
Jens Böke
Frank Püchner

Vision

From the historical perspective, the role of computer technology in the information age is comparable to the influence of mechanized production on industrial society, or that of land management on agrarian society. Changes in the tools of production have always changed society – and, by extension, architecture [77]. The increasing influence of digital technologies on the conception, development, and implementation of architectonic design has become particularly visible in recent years. Computers have now been introduced into almost all architecture firms, together with the appropriate programs and applications. Generative designing methods, building information modeling (BIM) and digital fabrication technologies are playing an increasingly significant role in the evolution of architectonic forms. The comprehensive representation of three-dimensional design concepts permitted by digital simulations, which also permit direct interaction with the virtual model during the design process – significantly expands the designer's awareness of spatial relationships. The computer is now capable of representing the whole designing and planning process, from the first concept visualization to the completed 3D building data set. This situation calls for an architect's classical task areas to be redefined. It requires architects to become familiar with a new language and to understand the methodology that lies behind digital designing. Recognizing the potential this offers promises more than simply new designing possibilities. Above all, it restores the architect to a central role in the whole architectural production process – from the initial idea to the completed building. This development holds out the prospect of simplifying processes in many areas of architectural development through the ability to respond more quickly to changes in the design, by saving time through automation, by increasing economic viability through this saving of time, by reducing the number of interfaces and potential sources of error, and through the ability to directly transfer the digital results into physical results through the use of CAD/CAM [78].

The computer is surely the most comprehensive and dynamic medium that architects have ever had at their disposal in completing their work. The possibilities inherent in digital designing methods bring new freedoms to the development of architecture. In order to benefit fully from this potential, however, those involved must recognize the computer's ability to function as an interactive instrument, and see its artificial intelligence as a creative asset. Professional handling of digital media allows architectonic quality to remain in the designer's area of responsibility from the first draft to realization while increasing the designer's influence on the future development of architecture.

Methodology

The three specimen projects described here are part of a series of student projects designed, developed, and implemented at the Detmold School of Architecture and Interior Design, Hochschule Ostwestfalen-Lippe, over the past few years with the aid of digital tools. These studies are prototypes intended to demonstrate the role of the methods described in the essay "Digital Architecture: From Drafting to Production" (p. 24) in specific projects from an

1

academic context. Aside from transmitting knowledge and expertise relating to parametric design, the assignments given to the students were geared to the on-site use of digital fabrication technologies. The students' work was created in the context of a continuous development process – from the first formal idea to the integration of functional, constructive, and material-specific aspects into the designing process to the manufacturing processes – incorporating diverse disciplines, workshops, and collaborations with external partners.

SunSys

Jens Böke's BA dissertation [79] was produced in response to the Detmold School's need to provide students on its campus with outdoor facilities, particularly for summer use. First, parameters for the design were established by analyzing on-site conditions using digital tools such as GPS tracking and sun-position analysis. In particular, existing patterns and structures of movement on-site, usage timeframes and alignment in relation to the course of the sun and to changing patterns of shade were used as source data for the designing work, into which they were incorporated generatively. Analysis of pedestrian routes and shade conditions were used to find the best possible location for the pavilion in the plaza between the main buildings. The values for the structure's graduated succession of open and enclosed sections were derived from the findings of the time-usage analysis and the sun analysis.

The profiles of the different usage areas, which give the spaces their form, were created with reference to the seating elements – chairs, benches, and deck-

2

2 Variations on the design, based on a parametric model

chairs. Users in the secluded zones are shielded from the bustle of the campus. These areas, however, do not feel shut-off or dark. Here, the roof part of the structure is open; in the areas of the pavilion designed to function as seating areas, it is closed. Based on the analysis, the sun vector for the day time span was used as the reference point for creating the openings in the structure.

The parametric structure model for the design that was ultimately put forward is based on a modeled output form. The individual surfaces of this output form were converted into a parametric definition, which was then given the appropriate structure. The pavilion was to be constructed from planar elements connected at an angle of 90°. The individual elements differ in shape, but can be manufactured on a CNC lathe using a single, unified principle. The structure of the openings is created solely by scaling the individual elements.

The fact that the structure is based on a formal principle means that SunSys should also be understood as a prototype for this principle. Given a different set of parameters, it would produce different major forms and different use functions, but the principle would remain the same. It is an illustrative example of the potential benefits of parametric designing and the resulting production processes. The individual building blocks, which also constitute the connective elements, are based on a formula that incorporates all parameters, but also permits endless variations in terms of combination, allowing for an ideal form with a high degree of diversity and precision [80].

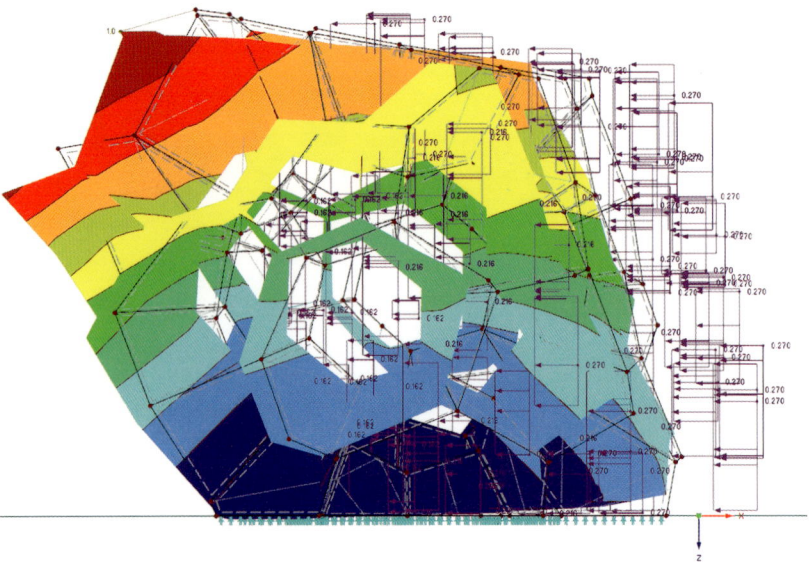

3

3 Simulation and optimization
of the load-bearing structure

Design to production

This architectural diploma dissertation by Frank Püchner took as its starting point the possibilities for producing curved surfaces using computer-assisted tools [81]. He investigated a number of construction systems in relation to digital construction variants, also implementing them as physical models. The first step was to produce the base geometry, a translation surface composed of sine curves, on the computer. This then served as the starting point for the investigation of a variety of production and construction variants.

During the next phase – the actual production phase – it emerged that changes and additions to the digital data model (in terms of values, materials, positions, details, and other factors) would be required in order to implement the digital model using computer-controlled machines. In particular, it was necessary to integrate readings on production tolerances, static requirements, and connection and join parameters, and the properties of the materials used (various wood types, hard foam) into the data set involved in the transition from planning to production.

To avoid having to produce the 3D model again from scratch as a result of these optimization measures, a parametric model permitting adaptation was developed using Rhinoceros 3D software. The digital model was duly parameterized with the aid of the Grasshopper plug-in [82], enabling modifications to be applied to the model in a holistic way. This allowed all the building blocks in the process to be simultaneously controlled and altered by means of a single cen-

4

4 Using laser-cutting technology
to produce a scale model

tral file. Grasshopper's visual programming also provided a template for practical implementation of the series of experiments. This resulted in a digital process chain capable of serving as the basis for a continuous development process, from the creation of the concept geometry to the refining of the 3D model to the realization. The parameterizing process allows any construction approach to be directly adapted and optimized, and to be evaluated in design terms.

In addition to the triangulation, horizontal layering, and insertion raster system production principles, Frank Püchner's architectural diploma dissertation incorporated the ZIP principle [83] as developed by Christoph Schindler, programmed as a functional data set. As a result, these digital tools do not relate solely to a single geometry – they also allow for the production of diverse single- and double-curved geometries.

Sparkler

Sparkler is a three-dimensional interpretation of the well-known study of proportions by Leonardo da Vinci, which shows the Vitruvian man within a circle and a square. Seen from the outside, this experimental pavilion [84] resembles an angular crystal, while its interior conforms to a perfect spherical geometry. These two basic forms are interconnected by the extended edges of a regular Archimedean form – a blunted icosahedron [85] – in such a way that the resulting spatial sculpture appears as an internally harmonious shape. This also means that the structure, which is composed of pentagons and hexagons, has formal similarities to the constructions of Richard Buckminster Fuller [86].

In the first stage of the designing process, a parametric geometrical model was constructed with the aid of the Rhinoceros/Grasshopper 3D modeling software. This geometrical model allowed the base geometry for both the interior and the exterior – a sphere and a block as space-enclosing volumes – and the various interface surfaces that ultimately create the form of the body to be placed in relation to one another. This 3D model, created to serve as a designing machine, made it possible for a large number of variations on the basic idea to be produced quickly, evaluated, and compared. Varying the sections on the external sides allows the pavilion to occupy seven different positions. As well as expanding the possibilities for use, this also alters the appearance of the sculptural structure in ways that are dependent on angles of perspective and on the contact area selected.

Additional information relating to production was added to the parametric model in order to prepare for production of the individual components using CNC technologies. In addition to optimized cutting to size of the panels (known as nesting), integrating the material thicknesses, and the required tolerances for assemblage, logistical aspects were a factor in the construction, deconstruction, and reconstruction of the digital model. In addition to helping to visualize the design spatially, a scale wood model created using the laser cutter (1:10) assisted in the preparation for and testing of the subsequent assemblage process.

Because the prototypical structure can be developed in an idealized process, allowing a fundamental understanding of the methods presented, the pavilion's typology presents a suitable field of experimentation for new spatial concepts. The 90 different geometrical multiplex panel formats from which Sparkler is composed are connected by more than 120 laser-cut force-fitted steel connections. This means that the structure, which is based on a buckyball, shows statically optimized load-bearing behavior, and also permits serial production of the identically shaped steel connectors.

Innovation

Innovations that develop in other branches of industry frequently find their way into architecture at a later date. As has been pointed out by Michael Hensel and Achim Menges, the introduction of CAD/CAM applications exemplifies this phenomenon in analogy to previous technological developments: "Long-standing, traditional ways of seeing and thinking predominate, coupled with polarized positions on how to respond to the new innovations" [87]. In spite of this apparent reluctance, the influence of the digital revolution on architecture is already clearly visible. As well as changing the formal shape of our built environment and the way we perceive it, the use of the computer has also changed the way the various parties involved in architectural construction operate. This makes it all the more important to adopt an active and critical attitude in following these developments.

In our twenty-first century, computer and information technology is fundamental. Digital information has become a basic requirement for the designing, planning, construction, and maintenance of buildings, and for uniting all the partners involved in the planning and realization of architecture. The real innovative potential of digital technologies for architecture lies in the possibility of bringing together the different processes in a consistent building data model [88]. Against this background, BIM is a digital planning method that interconnects all processes involved in the designing, planning, execution, and management of a building. All information is entered into a databank, and is linked associatively by means of a parametric system. Aside from graphical information relating to the building's geometry, this includes nongraphical information such as quantitative measurements, materials, time values, usages, and costs. Modifications made to any one of these levels – 3D levels, ground plan, or building component lists – are directly reflected on all other levels. Aside from comprehensively combining all information pertaining to the building for purposes of architecture planning, BIM also provides a connection or interface with other agencies involved in the planning process: for structural issues, for in-house systems in relation to building physics and facility management. The advantages of using this planning method include improvements to the planning process and to planning quality. The use of a shared database that is continually synchronized and immediate access to all current and relevant data results in a significant improvement in information exchange between those involved in the planning process.

At the designing phase, parametric models permit the investigation of different variants on a single principle. Constructing a data model of this kind defines the initial output situation, which can then be flexibly adapted as the process progresses. Knowledge of programming is indispensable for producing this model. Algorithms are created for the design's basic geometry; these permit the geometry and other aspects of the model, such as the materials and the construction, to be altered at a later stage. On this basis, the conditions for the design can be individually defined and manipulated. This fundamentally changes the designing method – and, consequently, the real-world implementation of the design. The impact of knowledge from other disciplines on architecture – such as IT and production technology – is increased. The really important issue will be the level of priority that is given to these areas and the aesthetic and functional results that are produced. As architects, it is incumbent on us to meet this challenge and to find an independent architectonic means of expression for our digital age.

Optimizing and Directing Processes

Xavier Ferrers
Thomas Braig
Jörn Tillmanns

Vision

The different architectural and engineering professions first took shape during the nineteenth century. Since then, little by little, architects have started to deal increasingly with form and engineers with building technology. During the twentieth century the what and how of a building have virtually become separated into different disciplines, Experts with specific training for each of the different fields now have to cooperate and to develop a suitable form of collaboration.

However, a building remains tied to the way it is built and to the materials in use. If the performance of buildings is to keep up with increasingly exacting ecological, sociocultural, and economic demands, technological advancements and new product developments are vital. Especially the facade of a building must perform a variety of key functions: it must give a building character, relate it to its surroundings, users, and function, and act as a complex membrane for energy exchange. The latter is a key issue when considering the adoption of light systems and materials, such as the curtain walls used for office and administration buildings. Current IT knowledge and tools allow us to assess these functions in advance, using 3D modeling, rendering, and energy and material performance simulations.

In the present day we have many innovative and high-performance technologies at our disposal; by intelligently combining and optimizing these modern applications to respond to technical, ecological, and economic issues, we

1

1 Concept sketch for double
skin envelope, New Masia FCB,
Barcelona, 2010, MCM Group-
Ferrés AC

could potentially significantly exceed existing standards. This strategy is particularly efficient where there has been an integrative planning process using computer simulations of energy consumption and costs, with product and planning experts and the future users and owners involved from the beginning. Programs such as the EcoCommercial Building Program (ECB), run by Bayer MaterialScience, offer precisely these services and this range of different types of expertise. The program brings together product and planning experts, creating a sustainable construction network that can incorporate cooperation between professional construction industry decision makers and developers, investors, and planners. Another option is to establish clear design processes under the direction of a specialist, in this case, the facade consultant.

Method

The basic requirement for clear design processes is the technical specification for the building and the facade that define the user comfort is an important issue in the architecture of buildings – especially when light-transparent facades are used. High-performance glass and other transparent materials combined with light and solar control systems can be used to create adaptable workspaces and living spaces capable of responding to a particular situation, orientation, climatic condition, and the time of day or night. The quantity and quality of light and solar radiation can be monitored to control temperature, humidity, and natural ventilation.

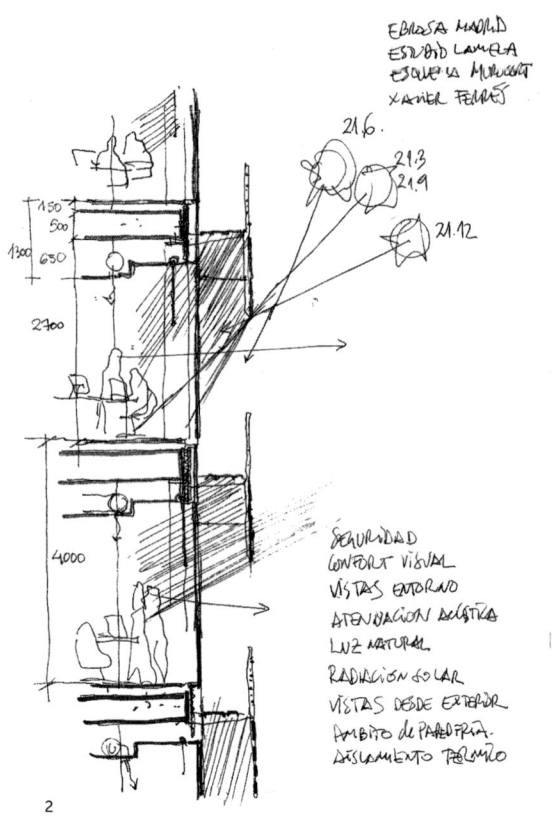

EBROSA MADRID
ESTUDIO LAMELA
ESQUELA MUNICPLT
XAVIER FERRES

SEGURIDAD
CONFORT VISUAL
VISTAS ENTORNO
ATENUACION ACUSTICA
LUZ NATURAL
RADIACION SOLAR
VISTAS DESDE EXTERIOR
AMBITO de PARED FRIA.
AISLAMIENTO TERMICO

2

2 Concept section for envelope,
EBROSA office building, Madrid,
2005, Estudio Lamela Arquitectos

The use of light facades that ignore the user's needs is unfortunately quite common. It is as if there was a new search in progress for a "global wrapping for buildings" that overlooks the context, repeats models with very few variations, and fails to consider the user's comfort or the construction's viability. One also frequently finds duplications and adoption of styles from a different latitude without appropriate thought. Performance expectations, economic viability, management models, and technical expertise are different for each project, and must be assessed holistically.

Unfortunately, the path from the world of conceptual ideas to constructed reality is long and arduous. There are many factors that determine the quality of the finished product. To improve their materialization, constructive proposals must be studied with special attention to detail. The design objectives at the start of any project are determined by:

> Requirements and expectations of the use and the users,
> Knowledge of the design process and industrial procedure,
> Material fabrications and transformation possibilities,
> Basic knowledge of construction techniques.

A study for a proposed sustainable supermarket within Germany provides an illustrative example of the successful application of this integrative planning process as carried out in the EcoCommercial Building Program (ECB). Both of the firms involved are founder members of the ECB-Program: the architecture firm Planquadrat and the energy engineering firm Bayer Technology Services.

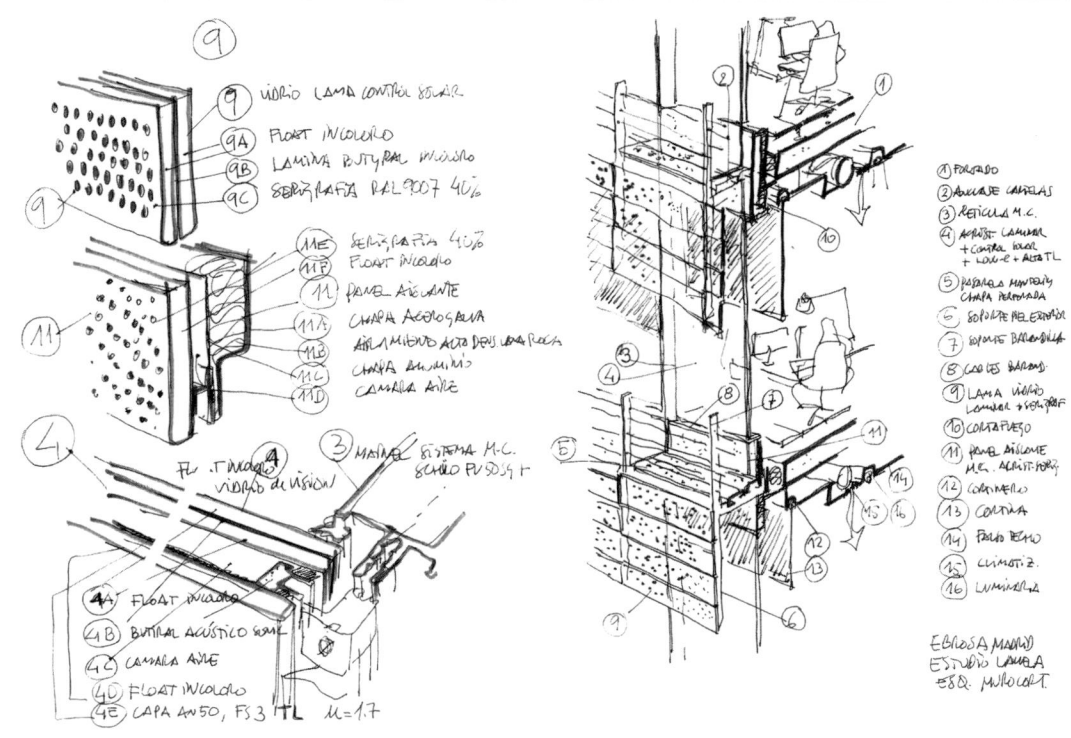

3 Concept sketch and details,
EBROSA office building, Madrid,
2005, Estudio Lamela Arquitectos

By combining innovative technologies that are already available and tested, this plan achieved annual energy savings of EUR 60,000 for a retail building with a usable space of 3,500m². The standard energy costs for a newly built conventional supermarket of EUR 23 per m² per year were brought down to EUR 6 per m² per year. The environment benefits from the reduction by more than half of carbon dioxide and nitric oxide emissions, and from the reduction by a half of SO_2 emissions, qualifying this study for the "Gold Certificate" of the German Sustainable Building Council (DGNB).

This building study shows that integrative planning and a highly individual and striking design are not mutually exclusive and that this design can also be realized with light building materials if the holistic building concept is adapted to that fact. In addition to making the sustainable character of the building clear to users (and playing a role in the corporate identity of the operator), the green roof helps to regulate the building's internal climate and the retention of rainwater. The northward orientation of the roof windows provides harmonious lighting for the interior by means of sunlight without direct exposure to the sun. At the same time, it allowed the surfaces to the rear to be used optimally for photovoltaic systems. The multiwall polycarbonate glazing is filled with nanogel, combining rupture safety and light weight with a high degree of transparency and exceptional insulation properties. The building's energy-efficient and resource-efficient outer shell is a major factor in its sustainable construction concept. Proven systems solutions based on heat-sealed plastic sheets ensure the sealing off of the green roof. Polyurethane – a high-performance insulating material – was used in all parts of the building shell. Lambda values of up to

4

4 Visualising the building:
sustainable building planning

0.024W/(m*K) were achieved in some application areas, enabling insulation performances up to 40% higher than those of other widely used insulation materials and allowing the superstructures to be slimmed down. Polyurethane maintains insulation performance at the same level for decades, and does not absorb water, meaning that even if a leak occurs there is no need to replace the insulation material. A layer of polyurethane can be up to 40% thinner than mineral wool alternatives and still provide the same amount of insulation. Due to its low specific weight, this material is also lighter by a factor of 7, enabling light constructions that are inexpensive and make sparing use of raw materials. Polyurethane is also sufficiently pressure-resistant to allow the roof to be walked on. The roof is supported by a framework system with a transverse orientation. Time-efficient and cost-efficient wall-construction systems based on wood/polyurethane and metal/polyurethane sandwich panels combine prefabricated construction capability with energy efficiency.

A striking photovoltaic facade is deployed on the building's entrance face. The solar modules in the front facade are arranged at the optimal angle, as are the other modules on the roof. The photovoltaic system is integrated into the polycarbonate light-construction plastic glazing, providing needed shade. The efficiency of the photovoltaics is further increased by the sunlight reflected from the moat in front of the entrance. The specific weight of polycarbonate is 10 times lower than that of glass, meaning that it can often be worked without heavy equipment and requires 30% less steel for its subconstruction – a saving on raw materials that also pays dividends in economic terms.

5

5 The building's construction
system

An intelligent mixture of conventional heat sources and renewable energy creates a comfortable, economic, and ecological building climate concept, with heat pumps combined with building component activation playing a major role. In spite of intensive utilization of daylight, artificial light sources are indispensable, as atmospheric accentuations or highly illuminated areas are necessary and desired. High-quality LED technologies have already proved their worth in supermarkets, lowering energy use by 75% or more. Polycarbonate envelopes make a significant contribution to ensuring the long usable life and efficient functioning of LEDs.

Floors are key interior architecture elements both in function and in design terms. No-joint systems based on polyurethane tolerate high loads and have a long, useful life. This permits less frequent maintenance work and generally simplifies cleaning. The environment benefits in total and over the life cycle from low waste production in the course of the renovation and from reduced use of cleaning materials.

Results

To obtain quality architecture, we must develop a design process featuring a correct choice of suitable facade systems and technical detail solutions that are consistent with a general building and building envelope concept. The proposed process can be applied to the design of new facades for new buildings, and also to existing building improvement:

6

6 Entrance side: Photovoltaic
facade with a belt of water
located in front of it

> Development of an idea from defined user needs, shapes, volumes, and
space. Feasibility studies must be made to clarify these ideas.
> Generation of a global architectural concept.
> Development of a facade or envelope concept integrated with the global
architectural concept. Fundamentally, the quality of a building is very
much defined by the success of the envelope and its correlation with the
building concept. This includes form, color, texture, light, shadow, and
transparency but also energy concepts, basic sections, and typological
decisions are made and envelope surface area and budget studies are
finalized. Interactions with Heating Venting and Air Conditioning (HVAC)
systems and structural analysis coordination are essential.
> Calculation of facade systems definitions and design details. This includes
the dimensions and therefore the mechanical and structural behavior of
facade elements, distances in relation to main structural elements, and
tolerances. We must also consider fireproofing regulations, fabrication
processes, assemblage, and maintenance. Diagrams and charts are used
to define the types of glass and other facade elements, compositions, and
performances.
> Technical specification of profile brands or design modifications, glass
products, other materials and their transformations, joints and seams, and
product compatibility within the envelope and with other elements of the
building.
> CAD detailing and drafting drawings are produced to verify the viability of
the facade and building concept. Complete drafting of all facade design
details is essential in order to minimize the element of risk occurring at the

7   8

7 Rendered image, Centre d'Alt
Rendiment Esportiu, Sant Cugat,
Competition 2010, TAC, Taller
d'Arquitectes col·laboradors,
SantCugat, Competition 2010,
TAC Eduard Gascónarquitectes

8 Pegaso Park office building,
under construction. Madrid,
2011, Estudio Lamela Arquitectos

execution stage. Often models in larger scale or 1:1 scale are necessary to prove the feasibility of the concepts.

Performance parameters are the reference point for every stage of the process. Every decision must be made in relation to components' technical behavior. To further reduce uncertainty, we must allocate time and resources to computer simulations and calculations, lab testing and on-site prototypes, and testing. If all these stages are applied consequently as done for the supermarket study, the overall budget is highly favorable: the energy costs are consistently Change to: approximately 75% lower than the values for a conventional building, and the emissions are approximately 50–75% lower than the comparison benchmark values. Integrative planning allows the sustainability of buildings to be improved using construction systems solutions that are available today and based on innovative light construction materials. They make it possible to optimize various building types to substantially exceed existing standards in terms of raw materials and energy efficiency, sociocultural compatibility, and economy.

Innovation

Mies van der Rohe said: "If inspiration is the moment previous to creation, the constructive detail is what makes it possible." The presented diagram is a cyclic process; a transit from the world of ideas to the executive project, from concept sketches to constructive detail. This is a process that has to be undertaken many times to ensure that the decisions made at each stage are consistent with

9

10

Energy costs [€/m²]	Conventional supermarket	Study sustainable supermarket
Oil	1,64	--
Electricity	15,84	2,03
Electricity (heat pump)	--	2,29
Gas	6,97	1,70
Total	**22,99**	**6,05**

11

Emissions [kg/m²]	Conventional supermarket	Study sustainable supermarket
CO_2	79	35
SO_2	11	6
NO_X	24	10

12

9 Building during construction, CMT 22@ office building, Barcelona, 2008, BatlleiRoigarquitectes

10 Facade prototype, Pegaso Park office building, Madrid, 2010, EstudioLamelaarquitectos

11 Energy costs balance sheet

12 Emissions values balance sheet

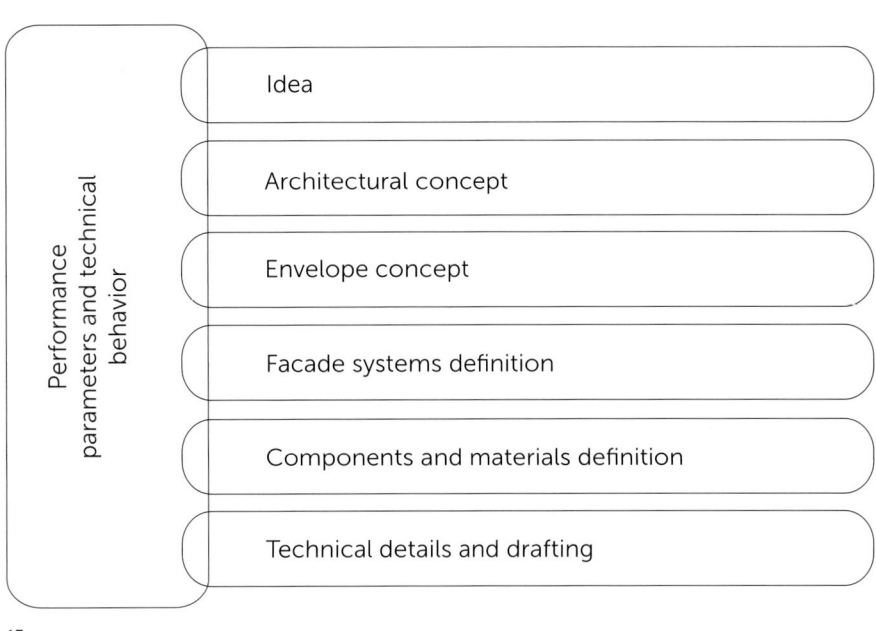

Performance parameters and technical behavior

- Idea
- Architectural concept
- Envelope concept
- Facade systems definition
- Components and materials definition
- Technical details and drafting

13

13 Cyclic process of designing

previous stages and with the project as a whole. It can easily be demonstrated that there is a direct relationship between the quality of a constructed envelope and an accurate design process. If the proposed cyclic design process is introduced correctly, it can lead to further innovations within architecture and building technology. For successful results, interdisciplinary technical collaboration is essential. Innovations that take place within each design aspect – e.g., components and materials – will be reflected in more innovative systems solutions.

Transfering
Technologies

The Printed Building Envelope

Holger Strauß

Vision

If we take advantage of the freedoms offered by Additive Manufacturing or AM for creating fine-detail construction components for the future, new approaches and fundamental ideas automatically present themselves [89]. The goal of the cooperative research project "Einfluss additiver Verfahren auf die Entwicklung von Fassadenkonstruktionen" (Influence of additive processes on the development of facade constructions), run jointly by the Hochschule Ostwestfalen-Lippe and the firm Kawneer-Alcoa (henceforth referred to as Kawneer) was to refine the results produced by these new freedoms through consultations with an industrial partner and to make them available for real applications.

The fundamentally different principles of manufacturing involved in Additive Manufacturing — also known as rapid prototyping, rapid manufacturing, solid free-form fabrication, layered fabrication, and by a number of other terms — permit the generation of closed geometries and free forms from 3D computer data. Its layer-by-layer production of components is in direct contrast to the subtractive process that has characterized our way of thinking as engineers — and by extension, the form and function of the technology we have developed — for the past 150 years. The AM process is already a tried and tested (production) tool in some parts of industry, but for architecture and construction technology, they are still undiscovered territory. It is in this area that the research project presented here aims to demonstrate the potential of these technologies. New lateral connections and new product approaches can be created only where there is the possibility of finding the right processual

1

2

technology for the appropriate application and of putting an interdisciplinary specialist team to work on it. The facade is a sensitive area in a building's overall concept, and is therefore open to a large number of development approaches. In this project, possible ways of using AM for an industrial facade system were considered for the first time [90]. In this text, Additive Manufacturing (AM) will be used as a synonym for additive fabrication processes.

Methods

Starting points

How does one begin to formulate a research approach for such a new area of application? In order to impose realistic limitations on the expectations, the following timeframe-related groups were used:

1. applications that could be implemented within one to five years, with results that could be directly realized using currently available technologies (at component level);
2. projects with a timeframe of five to ten years, with the intended results appearing to be attainable in the near future (subassembly and components level);
3. projects with a timeframe of twenty-five to thirty years, involving applications for which technologies available today were known to be inadequate (systems level).

3 4

3 Standard free-form connector.
Firm: Kolf & Molijn, the Netherlands

4 Standard free-form
element. Firm: Kolf & Molijn,
the Netherlands

This system of graduated timeframes allows the current state of production to be directly related to the requirements of a changed design ethos. Those involved in the project calculate that a process that begins with simple changes to standard components will develop into a unified approach, culminating in the "printed" building envelope.

Potential changes and improvements were arrived at by analyzing the components used in a standard facade system and by looking at the frequency of their use. The research project examined the use of materials, the reductions placed on geometries by the extrusion press production process, and the storage and the assembly of components. The overriding goal of the development work, however, was to produce a facade junction element (subassembly level).

From the very beginning of the project, it became clear that AM would have a considerable influence on the innovative development of components in construction technology. Additionally, it became clear that bringing the actual design of such parts to an adequate state of advancement would require significantly more time than had originally been envisaged, and that the quality of the end result would depend on the diversity of the specialists contained in the project team [90].

5 3D connector, rendering

6 3D connector, photograph

Results

The first result to be obtained that was viable given the current state of technology was an improved facade connector for Kawneer's standard AA-100 post-and-beam system. It incorporated digital planning tools, an individualization of the facade geometry and a structural improvement to the post-and-beam connections.

Today's "AA-100 System" incorporates a connector profile for nonorthogonal splices. Due to the geometrical restrictions imposed by the extrusion process, however, this component does not satisfy all requirements for a connector of this type. The extrusion tools are optimized for the process in the first stage, and are not optimized for the actual profile use as a component until the second phase. The manufacture process, then, places constraints on the geometry of the extruded profiles, but also on the minimum quantity that must be provided for, and therefore also places constraints on storage and on throughput values.

In the specific case of the post-and-beam connector, the angle at which the post lies atop the beam can be varied. However, the low contact area and the nondefined position of the screw channels result in a load transfer in the connection that is many times smaller than in the equivalent orthogonal system.

The AM design for an improved connector integrates all angles and drilled holes digitally. This allows precisely gauged connections for every facade junction point to be planned by means of a parametric model and manufactured using

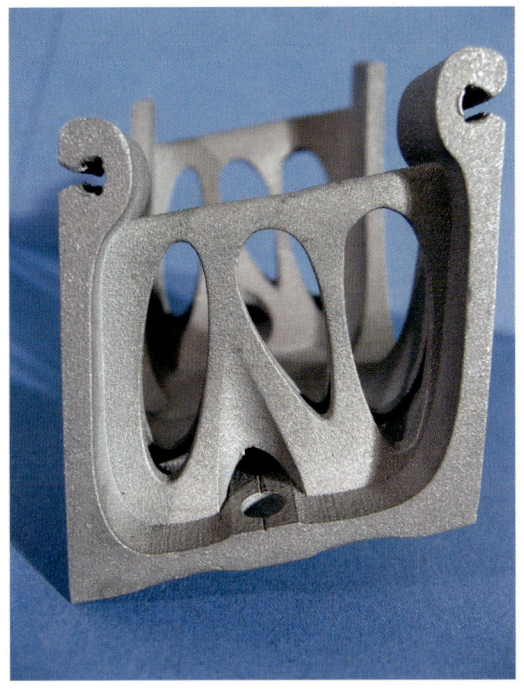

7

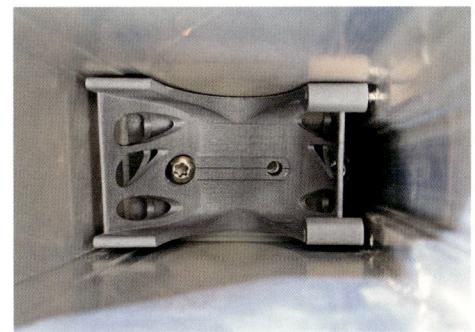

8

7 3D connector, detail

8 DMLS construction
component in beam profile

AM. In the case of the component presented here, the shape was optimized through the "digital" removal of material not required for functionality, saving 25 percent of materials compared to the standard component (defined by Mattheck as the "soft kill option" [91]). The AM process will produce only the quantity of connectors that is required (on-demand production). The "digital connector" can be installed using the standard post-and-beam system components, in a similar manner to the orthogonal construction style. As the installation situation remains unchanged, the same tools and additional parts are used for the modified facade as for a standard one. The beam profiles are processed using the CNC lathe to create the precise angle, using information from the deformation data.

The optimization potential for this connector is good because the component geometry is changed to reflect deformations in the facade. The digital programming of the angles required combined with the reduction in materials consumption and the improvement in performance properties demonstrate the added value associated with AM. This "digital" connector is the first prototype to be manufactured additively in stainless steel. Although it has not progressed past the first stage of development, it demonstrates the potential and the ways in which drafts and performance can be changed.

These first optimized components yielded a second approach to fulfilling the predefined goals of the project: a "one-off" solution for a deformed beam-and-post facade which demonstrates the current state of advancement in "Direct Metal Fabrication" (DMF) – the use of additive processes to manufacture

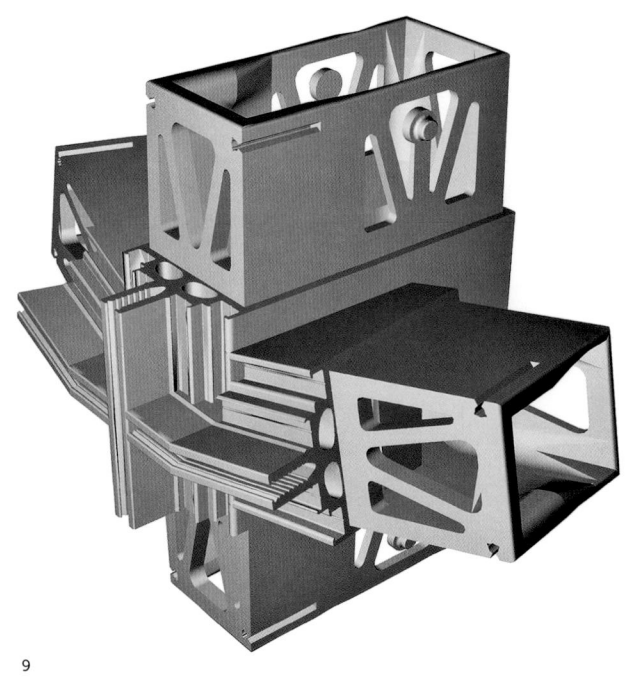

9

9 Nematox II, rendering

components in metal **[92]**. This initiative led to the development and realization of a digitally planned and additively manufactured facade node – the Nematox.

This component took all the advantages of the previously developed connector a step further, resulting in a node point that can be directly manufactured with the correct dimensions and to possess the advantages described above in greater measure. The merging of the post and the beam profile means that only perpendicular saw cuts are necessary for the assemblage of the facade. This optimizes the cutting on the profile, thus easing assembly. This also makes the water conduits' transit from the beam into the post's channels easier, improving the system technically. All the additional parts from the existing system can also be used for the deformed facade **[90]**.

Project evaluation

The use of an additive process as a production strategy adds a further branch to the digital process chain ("file-to-factory"). AM facilitates the ideal situation for CAD/CAM production by making it possible to incorporate information directly from the digital design process into the design component. For a construction assignment concerning an existing building, this might involve measurements that take account of deformation, but for a new building plan, it could also be a free geometry that deviates from the orthogonal system **[93]**. A direct – i.e., automated – implementation allows free-form components to be manufactured to the same quality as an orthogonal system, including all angles and the necessary connecting elements. In the case of the AA-100 facade recorded

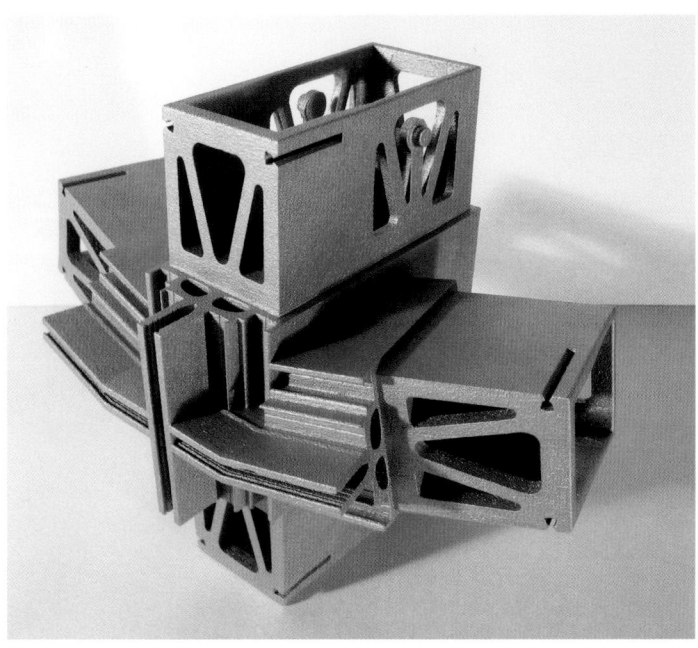

10

11

10 Nematox II, photograph

11 Nematox II, mock-up

here, the digitally adapted connectors between post and beam would optimally transmit all loads from the beam to the post, while accepting all seals and bonding agents to the same standard as the orthogonal system. The Nematox node also allows curved facades to be optimized in terms of cutting and a secure system to be implemented. The risk of faulty connections and sealing layers is minimized. Digital planning and manual implementation enter into a new relationship – a kind of digital craftsmanship.

Innovation

Potential applications in facade construction

Of itself, Additive Manufacturing offers designers and engineers many possibilities for reinterpreting existing objects. The projects described here extend this to facades – a whole new area of application for AM. In addition to the results of the project, a clear picture has been created for how research into this area might be continued. Development of the presented AM facade prototypes to a point at which they can be used in a project for the first time would represent a true milestone in construction technology. The project made it clear that intensive engagement with the new technologies is needed to highlight the important questions and to bring highly specific options for further research to light. Knowledge of technical possibilities and limitations is essential to further development – especially of applications in building envelopes. For those considering deploying these methods in the facade industry, the available DMF metals are interesting potential building materials because their material properties are sufficiently known. The ability to import established facts creates a greater degree of confidence for the developer in terms of dimensions and stability. The benefits that first recommended this technology for use and that originally led to the project's being conceived (light construction, free forms, savings on materials, integrated functions etc.) make existing drafting strategies and thought models obsolete. They could lead to a radical reinterpretation of existing systems, components, details, and design approaches.

By contrast, when rapid technologies were invented in the 1980s, they were initially used purely for manufacturing demonstration models – a process known as rapid prototyping. All the work within the market today, however, is geared toward manufacturing products that support actual use, and not the manufacture of prototypes.

There are currently no official regulations or quality standards for AM technology products. If standardized production is envisaged, a general building supervision approval is required for the materials and products used. In the area of construction technology in particular, standardized components and load cases are defined with reference to standardized construction components. As construction is always concerned with the safety of the user, certification and assessable material properties – and therefore assured accountability – is a priority goal of the development process [90], [94].

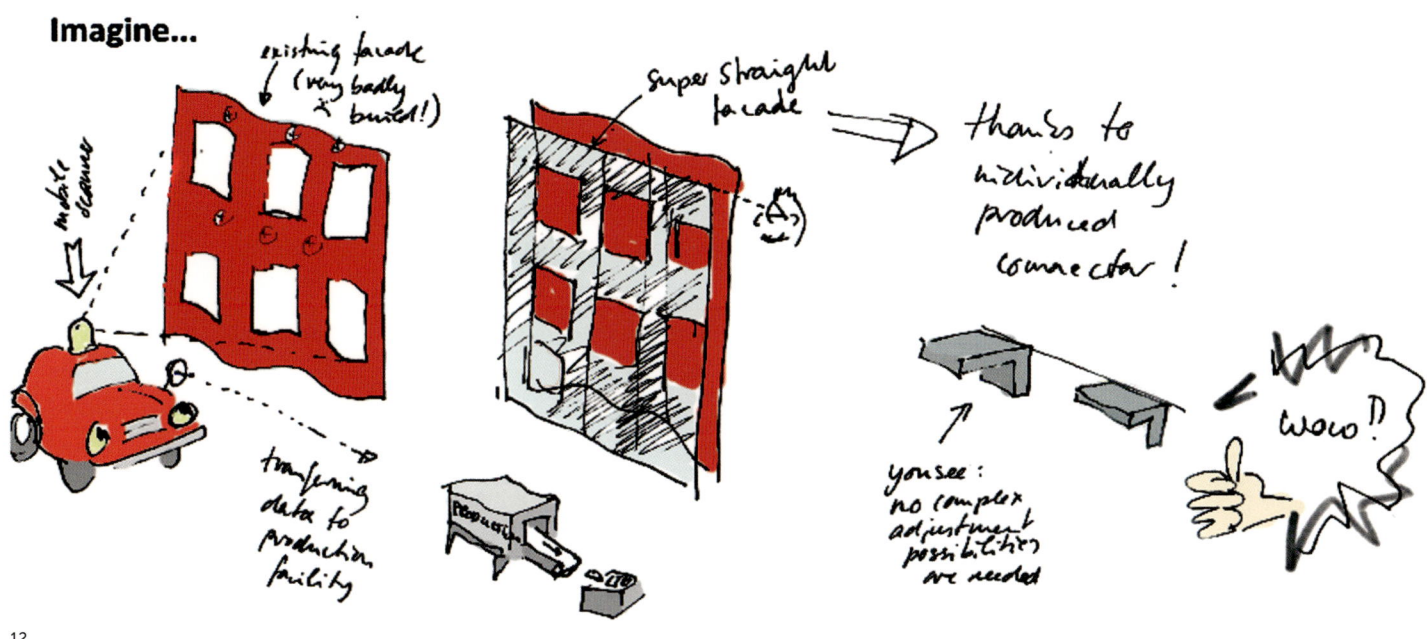

Imagine...

12

12 "Zero Tolerance Refurbishment Facade" principle, from "Imagine RAPIDS"

The end result of the research and theory can be summed up by saying that there is the prospect of a broad field of applications beyond the current limitations. The corresponding change in our thinking began long ago – CAD/CAM, file-to-factory, and digital materials are becoming established as current keywords, and the first solid results are now being demonstrated. The evolution of the technologies is extremely rapid, making a more intuitive use of AM a real prospect. It has also become clear that there are still hurdles to be overcome on the road to "real" application of AM if the technology is to be exploited to its full potential. These hurdles, however, are largely technical in character and are not limitations that are inherent in the AM system.

In future, the constructs of planners and architects will have to be "fit for function rather than fit for production" (Wilhelm Meiners, Fraunhofer Institute for Laser Technology [95]).This turns the well-known, secure framework of engineering knowledge and the architectural doctrines of the past hundred years on its head.

Direct Glass Fabrication

Lisa Rammig

Vision

Digital technologies largely determine contemporary lives, and their importance continues to grow in various sectors. Starting in the 1970s with the first personal computers, these technologies have significantly influenced economy and society. Computer technologies provide the possibility of mass-production processes, where manual labor is not required and accuracy and optimization can be guaranteed. The development of digital fabrication moves from mass-production to more customized and individualized fabrication. It is possible to create the perfect product without reverting to single-piece – handcraft – manufacturing. The customer becomes part of the production again; the product grows to their taste.

While the direct fabrication of materials such as plastics or metals are now a sophisticated technology (known as Additive Manufacturing, or AM), the direct fabrication of glass, perhaps one of the most fascinating building materials, is almost unexplored. Glass is strong but brittle, heavy yet looks lightweight, and it is transparent. These properties have made glass an important component of our built environment. Several types of glass, such as laminated and insulated glazing, coated, curved, and free-formed glass panes were developed rapidly after the float glass process was invented. Besides the progress in glass production, structures have also been further developed to increase a transparent architectural appearance. Current architecture is strongly influenced by digital media and 3D modeling software, giving us the possibility to create almost anything. In turn, this has developed the need for better-performing glass ele-

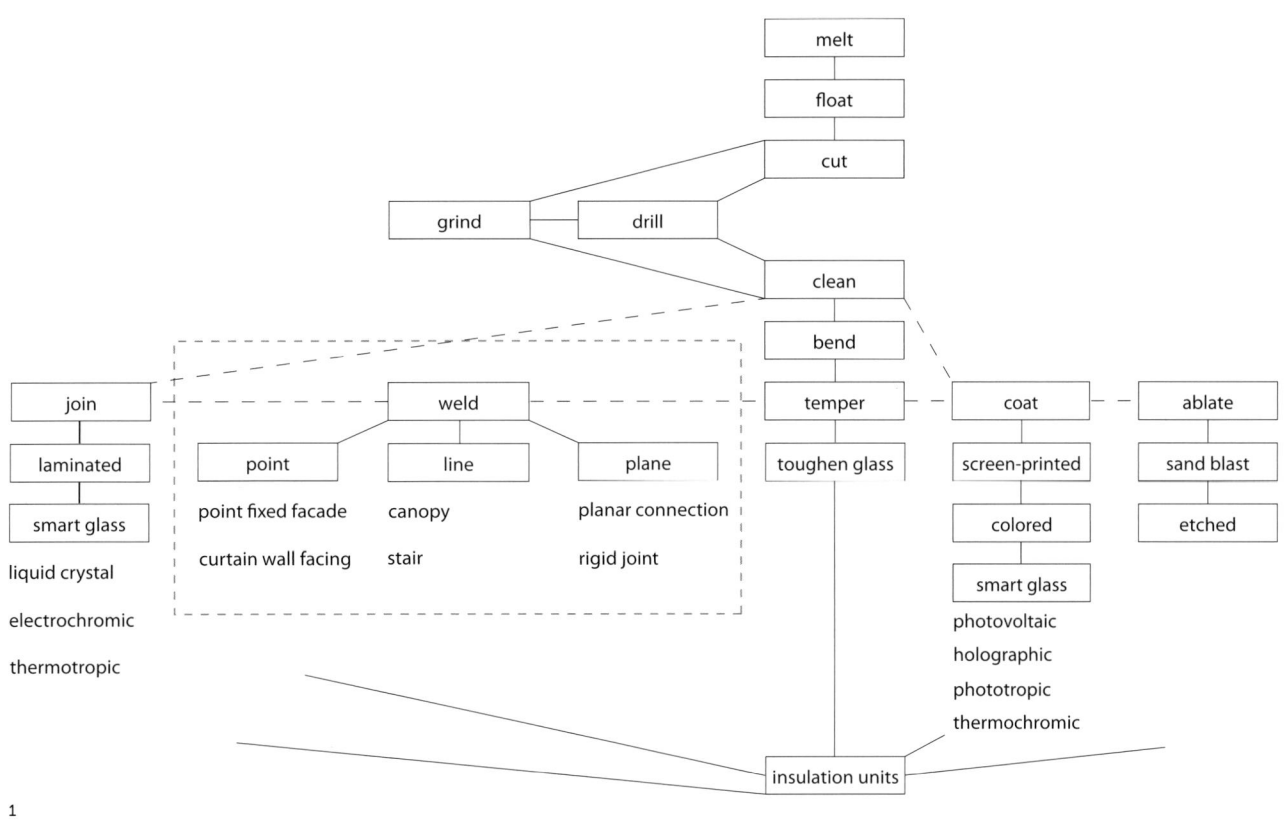

melt → float → cut

grind → drill

clean → bend → temper → toughen glass

join → laminated → smart glass

liquid crystal
electrochromic
thermotropic

weld → point, line, plane

point: point fixed facade, curtain wall facing
line: canopy, stair
plane: planar connection, rigid joint

coat → screen-printed → colored → smart glass

photovoltaic
holographic
phototropic
thermochromic

ablate → sand blast → etched

insulation units

1

1 Schematic diagram:
glass processing

ments and connections. Free-formed glass panes, each one different to the other, might fit perfectly together, but are produced individually. At this point the question arises: why not use AM for glass production? Direct glass fabrication (DGF) would give the possibility to produce free-formed transparent building parts, without the complexity of the conventional steps of production.

This article discusses the opportunities and limitations of technology with respect to material properties, current technologies, design parameters, recent developments, practical testing, and possible areas of further research.

Method

Glass: the material

Glass can be described physically as a rigid inorganic silicate product of amorphous nature. In contrast to crystalline materials it is characterized by its isotropy, which means that all properties or measured values are the same in each direction of the structure. Conventional glass such as soda-lime glass consists of silica sand, lime, and soda. Properties such as stiffness and color can be adapted by the addition of other materials.

Compared to other substances like metal or plastics, which are defined by their chemical affinity, glass is described by its structural composition, which must be seen irrespective of the chemical composition. The advantageous properties

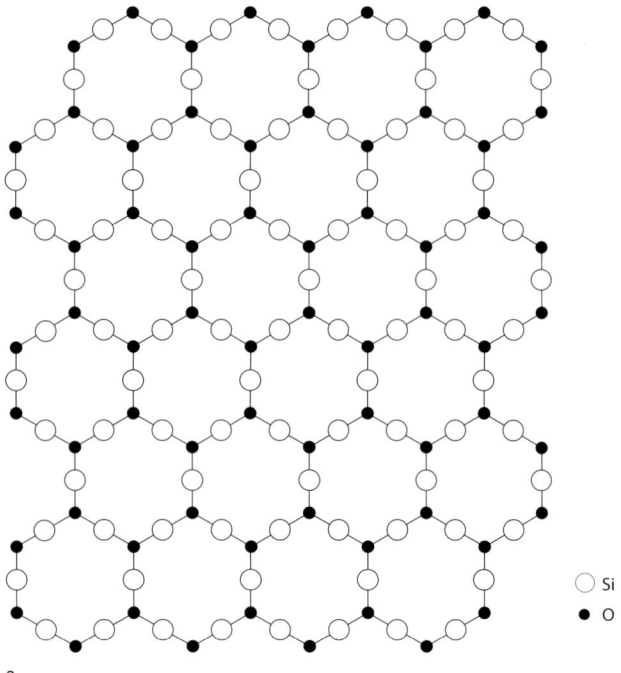

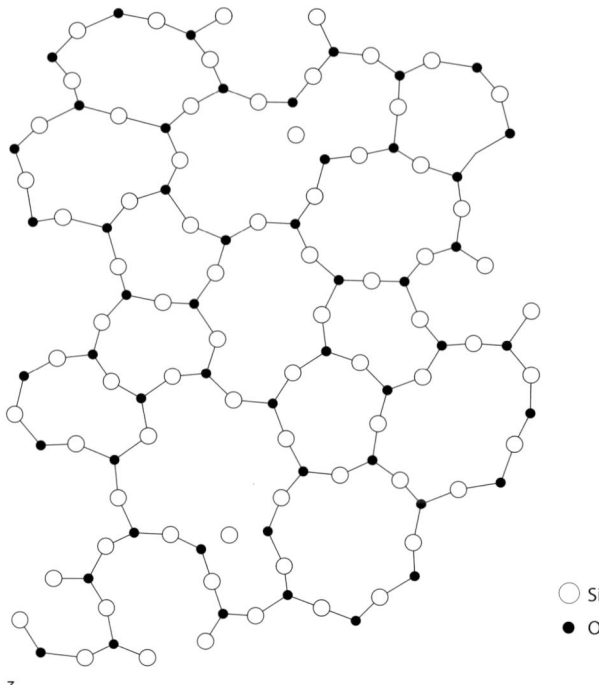

Si
O

Si
O

2

3

2 Soda-lime glass

3 SiO$_2$ crystal, 2D

of glass such as light transmittance, thermal behavior, and solidity result from its molecular structure. Silica glass has the simplest structure, as it consists solely of silicon dioxide. While the structure of a silica crystal is sorted, the molecular composition in its glass state is unsorted, and therefore it is not a crystalline structure. The material seems to be liquid but does not tend to creep or flow.

The high proportion of silica sand (around 75 percent) expresses the hardness, strength and brittleness of the material. A brittle material fails or breaks after minimal deformation. The composition of the glass is a fundamental factor of the viscosity of the melt and the properties of rigid glass. As described, pure silica glass tends to crystalize but has a very low coefficient of linear thermal expansion, which makes it resistant to temperature differences and thermal shocks.

Technical parameters for DGF

The technical parameters governing the development of direct glass fabrication (DGF):

> The coefficient of linear thermal expansion is an important value for the applications of glass, especially for analyzing the material with respect to additive manufacturing processes.
> The theoretical strength of the glass expresses stiffness as a result of the bond strength of individual components, which unrealistically assumes a crack-free glass.

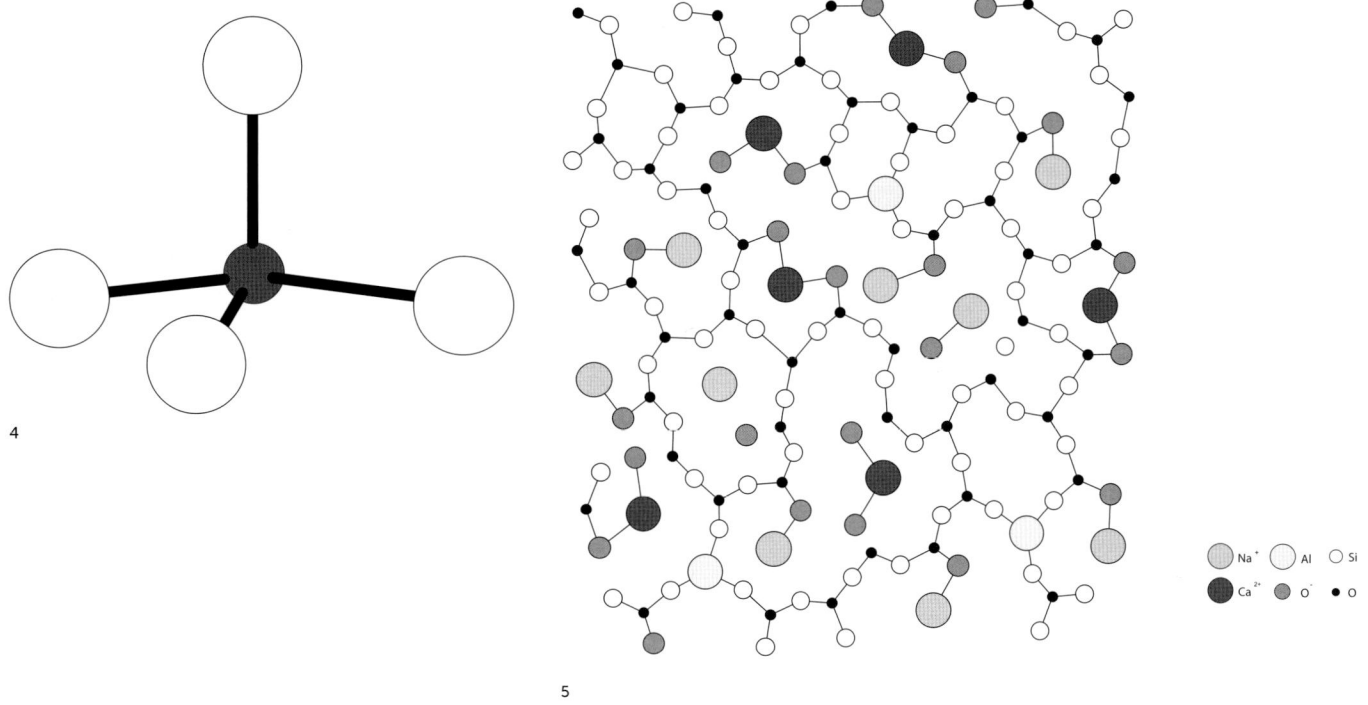

4

5

Na⁺ Al Si
Ca²⁺ O⁻ O

4 SiO$_4$, 3D

5 SiO$_2$ glass, 2D

> The practical strength takes into account such cracks and is therefore significantly lower. This strength value is crucial for the dimensioning of components.

Borosilicate glass is primarily used in the chemical and pharmaceutical industries because it offers better chemical resistance and a lower coefficient of linear thermal expansion, which is important to be able to heat contained liquids with a burner. This significantly enhances its resistance to large temperature differences induced by the additive fabrication process.

Another important factor is the viscous performance of the material. When a crystalline substance is heated, it will melt at a particular temperature, and become liquid. In contrast, glass does not have a melting point; it softens continuously under the influence of temperature. The organized molecular structure of a crystal produces a hard solid material, while glass has an irregular structure and therefore behaves like a cooled liquid. For a DGF addition onto a conventional fabricated glass sheet, the whole pane of glass must be heated to a uniform temperature, which is limited by the thermal shock resistance of the glass.

Practical application

A practical test was carried out to evaluate the possible processes of AM glass technology. The material layer arrangement, related to temperature, is fabricated using a welding process. To verify the quality of jointing, tubes and rods were welded to glass panes, followed by panes, layers, and points. These were

6

7

6 Manual welding process

7 Connection after
mechanical testing

made by heating a glass rod, elongating it to a thin wire and then welding it onto a pane of glass. The connected layers must have a constant high temperature such that bonding with the next layer is possible. Borosilicate glass was used, as its properties are suitable for welding processes.

To simulate the process of AM, the glass panes were laid in a fire-resistant box and preheated using a burner. The joints were welded with this same burner. After joining the glass, the panes were then annealed in a ceramic oven, where the material can be cooled slowly from working temperature to room temperature, from 800°C down to 20°C within twenty hours.

Results

Different types of connections were manufactured to compare and evaluate atomic bonding. Firstly, the behavior of glass-glass connections was tested and the degree of precision to which they could be made. The applications of layer-by-layer fabrication were then completed to simulate an industrial additive manufacturing process.

Testing of the welded connections showed that the failure of the material generally occurs within the region of the original material, confirming that the connections are stiffer than the original material.

The implementation verifies that it is possible to manufacture glass-glass connections with AM processes layer by layer, generating stiff connections. The

8

8 Manual process of
layer glass welding

question arises of how such a production method could be used in architecture or the facade industry and what products it could develop.

To develop architectural applications from basic production principles, a glass point fixing was designed such that it can be attached to the glass pane by an additive process. This was then fabricated and tested for numerous connections.

When compared to conventional point fixations, one of the main advantages is that the quantity and size of fixings can be determined individually for each pane. Attachments are optimized based on the dead load, wind load, and other influences. The most important advantage of the point fixing however, is the removal of the need to drill the glass panes, so that no stresses are induced, and thermal losses are reduced as there is no thermal bridging. The penetration of the outer pane is avoided, which means that the thermal separation of the facade is uninterrupted. This is of significant importance for the Northern European climate, now more than ever with current energy-saving regulations and sustainability considerations.

Innovation

Developments in AM technologies for glass, one of the most aesthetically pleasing materials, are still in the early stages. Examining material properties, common technologies, and analyzing the parameters governing DGF the following conclusions can be made:

Fabrication technologies are available but must be adapted for the properties of glass. This research tries to show these fabrication abilities by moving away from computer-controlled additive processes to a manual process.

The major problem when dealing with larger panes of glass is that they have to be heated carefully to avoid breakage of the material. The behavior of the glass can be customized by modifying properties such as viscosity, thermal linear expansion coefficient, and the resulting maximum thermal shock resistance. For the fabrication of large products, special heating and cooling components are required to provide the object with uniform heat. Partial heating of the glass would result in material breakages caused by thermal stresses.

The developed point fixing technique highlights the applicability of DGF to facade design. Producing a fixing that connects the glass panes to the primary facade without penetration of the outer pane can lead to new opportunities in facade construction. It would be possible to construct facades without thermal breaks and without the visual disturbance of conventional point fixings. It has been shown that the additive manufacturing process for producing glass is feasible. The results also encourage further research to be undertaken within the field so that products can be developed that are truly representative of the technological advances.

9

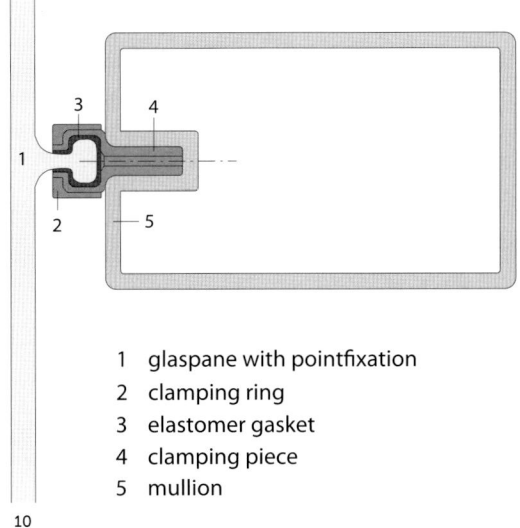

10

1 glaspane with pointfixation
2 clamping ring
3 elastomer gasket
4 clamping piece
5 mullion

9 Glass point fixing

10 Detail of glass point fixing

Notes

Human-Centered Design

[1]   Gropius, Walter. *Scope of Total Architecture*. New York: First Collier Books, 1962.

[2]   Nefiodow, Leo A.: *Der sechste Kondratieff*. 6th, updated edition. St. Augustin, 2006.

[3]   Bürdek, Bernhard E.: *Design: Geschichte, Theorie und Praxis der Produktgestaltung*. Cologne: DuMont 1991.

[4]   Rittel, Horst W. J.; Webber, Melvin M.: "Dilemmas in a General Theory of Planning." *Policy Sciences* 4 (1973): 155–169.

[5]   Simon, Herbert A.: *The Sciences of the Artificial*, 3rd edition. Cambridge, MA: MIT Press. 1969/2001.

[6]   Archer, Bruce: "The Nature of Research." *Co-Design Journal* 107 (1995): pp. 6–13.

[7]   Alexander, Christopher; Ishikawa, Sara; Silverstein, Murray: *Pattern Language*. New York: Oxford University Press, 1977.

[8]   Caan, Shashi, *Rethinking Design and Interiors. Human Beings in the Built Environment*. London: Laurence King Publishing, 2011.

[9]   Romero-Tejedor, Felicidad; Jonas, Wolfgang, eds.: *Positionen zur Designwissenschaft*. Kassel: Kassel University Press, 2010.

[10] Reichhardt, Ulrike: "Designwisschenschaft und Planungswissenschaft," in: Hugentobler, Hans Kaspar et al, eds. *Designwissenschaft und Designforschung. Ein einführender Überblick*. Lucerne: Lucerne University of Applied Arts and Sciences, 2010, pp.85–92.

[11] Papanek, Victor: *Design for the Real World: Human Ecology and Social Change*. London: Thames & Hudson, 1972.

[12] Eames, Charles and Ray: *India Report*. Ahmedabad: National Institute of Design (NID), 1958/1997.

[13] Pottgiesser, Uta: "Interior Design as an Academic Discipline in Germany," in: *Journal of Interior Design* 36, no. 4 (2011).

[14] Verganti, Robert: *Design-driven Innovation. Changing the Rules of Competition by Radically Innovating What Things Mean*. Cambridge, MA: Harvard Business Press, 2009.

[15] Norman, Donald, A.: "Human-Centered Design Considered Harmful," *Interactions* 9, no. 4 (2005): pp. 14–19.

[16] König, Katharina: "Architektur- und Raumwahrnehmung," Ph.D. dissertation, University of Paderborn, 2013.

[17] Pottgiesser, Uta; Hemmerling, Marco: "Spatial Perception in Real and Virtual Environments Methodology and Case Studies," in: *Proceedings DDSS-Design Decision Support Systems Conference*, Eindhoven, Netherlands, 2010.

[18] Bachelard, Gaston: *Poetik des Raumes*. Munich: Hanser, 1975.

[19] Buchanan, Richard: "Wicked Problems in Design Thinking," *Design Issues* 8, no. 2 (1992): pp. 5–21.

[20] Buck, Alex: *Dominanz der Oberfläche: Betrachtung zu einer neuen Bedeutsamkeit der Gegenstände*. Basel, Berlin: Birkhäuser, 2002.

[21] Dekomien, K., Baade, J. C., Kortüm, C., Riegel, A.: *Sensorische Gütebestimmung von Oberflächen (insbesondere Holzoberflächen)*. Final Report EFRE 290001602. Lemgo: Hochschule Ostwestfalen-Lippe, 2010.

[22] Chesbrough, H. W.: *Open Innovation: The New Imperative for Creating and Profiting from Technology*. Boston: Harvard Business School Press, 2003.

Digital Architecture: From Design to Production

Article based on a publication by Marco Hemmerling in *der architekt* 6/2011 and a publication by Ulrich Nether in *Augmented Reality*, Munich 2011.

[23] McLuhan, Marshall: *Die magischen Kanäle – Understanding Media*. Düsseldorf: Econ-Verlag, 1970.

[24] Zellner, Peter: "Grübelei über den trügerischen Zauber einer soften, digitalen Architektur: Oder: Wie ich lernte, mir keine Sorgen mehr zu machen und den Blob zu lieben." In: Cachola Schmal, Peter: *Digital Real – Blobmeister – First Built Projects*. Basel, Berlin: Birkhäser, 2002, p. 38.

[25] Hemmerling, Marco; Tiggemann, Anke: *Digital Design Manual*. Berlin: DOM Publishers, 2011.

[26] Nether, Paradigmenwechsel im Design, in Martin-Ludwig Hofmann (ed.): Design im Zeitalter der Geschwindigkeit, Munich 2010, p. 82.

[27] Antoine de Saint-Exupéry: *Terre des Hommes, III: L'Avion*. Paris: Gallimard, 1939.

[28] Further information on the content and structure of the postgraduate master's degree in computational design and construction at the Detmold School of Architecture and Interior Design, based at the Hochschule Ostwestfalen-Lippe can be found at: www.m-cdc.de.

[29] Hemmerling, Marco, ed.: *Augmented Reality – Mensch, Raum und Virtualität*. Munich: Wilhelm Fink Verlag, 2011.

[30] Rashid, Hani; Couture, Lise Anne: *Asymptote: Flux*. London: Phaidon Press, 2002.

Facade Road Map

[31] http://de.wikipedia.org/wiki/Innovation Accessed December 26, 2010.

[32] Meijs, Maarten; Knaack, Ulrich: *Prinzipien der Konstruktion: Bauteile und Verbindungen*. Basel, Berlin: Birkhäuser, 2009.

[33] http://www.spiegel.de/netzwelt/tech/0,1518,443717,00.html Accessed on December 26, 2010.

[34] Knaack, Ulrich: *Konstruktiver Glasbau*. Cologne: Müller, 1998.

[35] Gauzin-Müller, Dominique: "Eine Architektur der Harmonie und Poesie," in: *Behnisch und Partner – Bauten und Projekte 1952–1992*. Stuttgart: Hatje, 1992.

[36] Knaack, Ulrich; Klein, Tillman; Bilow, Marcel; Auer, Thomas: *Prinzipien der Konstruktion: Fassaden*. Basel, Berlin: Birkhäuser, 2007.

[37] Compagno, Andrea: *Intelligente Glasfassaden*. Basel, Berlin: Birkhäuser, 1995.

[38] Beim, Anne; Nielsen, Jesper; Vibaek, Kaper Sánchez: *Three Ways of Assembling a House*. Copenhagen: Arkitektens Forlag, 2009.

[39] Knaack, Ulrich; Klein, Tillman; Bilow, Marcel: *Imagine 01: Facades*. Rotterdam: 010 Publishers, 2008.

[40] Knaack, Ulrich; Klein, Tillman: *The Future Envelope 3: Facades – The Making Of*. Amsterdam: IOS Press, 2010.

[41] Stratton, Roy; Mann, Darrell: "Systematic Innovation and the Underlying Principles Behind TRIZ and TOC," *Journal of Material Processing Technology* 139 (2003): pp. 120–126(7).

Curved Planes

[42] http://www.glunz.de

[43] http://www.danielmichalik.com, cf. Reis, Dalcacio and Wiedemann, Julius, eds.: *Product Design in the Sustainable Era*. Cologne: Taschen, 2010.

[44] http://www.dukta.com, cf. Sauer, Christiane: "Flexibles Holz," in md (January 2010): pp. 70–71.

[45] Steffen, Dagmar, ed.: *C_Moebel: digitale Machart und gestalterische Eigenart*. Frankfurt: Anabas-Verlag, 2003, p. 178.

[46] http://www.rokarch.com, cf. Hensel, Michael; Kraft, Sabine and Menges, Achim: "Simple Systems, Complex Capacities – Die Ergebnisse des ARCH+ Wettbewerbs," in: *ARCH+*, nos. 196/197 (2009): pp. 2–5.

[47] Stevens, William Cornwall; Turner, Norman: *Wood Bending Handbook*. London: H.M.S.O., 1970.

[48] Taylor, Zachary: *Wood Bender's Handbook*. New York: Sterling, 2001.

[49] holz 21 2007, Design Plus Material Vision 2007, iF Material Award 2008, M Technology Award 2008 SILVER, Holz bewegt 2011.

[50] Schindler, Christoph: "ZipShape – A Computer-Aided Fabrication Method for Bending Panels without Molds," in: *Architecture "in computro"* [26th eCAADe Conference Proceedings], Antwerp 17–20 September 2008, pp. 795–802.

References: The text reproduced here is an extensively reworked translation of the original publication: Schindler, Christoph, and Salmerón Espinosa, Margarita: "ZipShape Moldless Bending II – A Shift from Geometry to Experience," in: *Respecting Fragile Places* [29th eCAA De Conference Proceedings], Ljubljana 21–24 September 2011, pp. 477–484.

Total Building Envelope

[51] Lo, S.; Ledbetter, Stephen: Centre for Windows and Cladding Technology (CWCT), University of Bath, 2010.

[52] Heusler W.: "Nachhaltige Gebäudehüllen – Anforderungen und Lösungsansätze für Büros," in Spath, Dieter; Bauer, Wilhelm; Rief, Stefan: *Green Office – Ökonomische und ökologische Potenziale nachhaltiger Arbeits- und Bürogestaltung*. Wiesbaden: Gabler Verlag, 2010.

Engineers Construct Art

[53] EN12600:2002, Glass in buildings – Pendulum test – Impact test method and classification for flat glass.

[54] DS/INF 119:2006, Guidelines for the selection and use of safety glass – Personal safety.

[55] Eurocode 1991:2002 parts 1–5.

[56] prEN14373-3, Nov 2005, Glass in building – Determination of the strength of glass panes – Part 3: General method of calculation and determination of strength of glass by testing.

[57] NS3510:2006, Sikkerhetsglass i bygg – krav til klasser i ulike bruksområder.

[58] CWCT TN66, Safety and Fragility of glazed roofing – guidance on specification and testing.

[59] Henriksen, Thomas: "Aros, Your Rainbow Panorama, by Olafur Eliasson" GPD, Tampere, 2009.

Acknowledgements: Special thanks to Studio Olafur Eliasson, SHL architects, and ArtEngineering for their contributions to this article.

Open Innovation

[60] Rosenkranz, Nicole; Enkel, Ellen; Foltin, Eckard: *Bayer MaterialScience: Market-Pull durch Open Innovation*. Düsseldorf: Symposion Publishing, 2010.

[61] Pricken, Mario: *Kribbeln im Kopf*. Mainz: Verlag Hermann Schmidt, 2007.

Connections and Layers

[62] DIN EN ISO 354: Akustik – Messung der Schallabsorption in Hallräumen (ISO 354:2003)

[63] Fuchs, Helmut V.: *Schallabsorber und Schalldämpfer*. Berlin: Springer, 2007.

[64] ISO 354:1985: Acoustics – Measurement of absorption coefficients in a reverberation room.

[65] Pottgiesser, Uta; Knaack, Ulrich; Strauß, Holger, eds.: *Facade2011 – Super Green. Tagungsband*. Detmold: 2011.

Wohn-Vision-2020

[66] Fleischhauer, Mark; Wriedt, Verena: *Wohn-Vision-2020. Möbel und Objekte aus gebrauchten Materialien*. Detmold: Hochschule Ostwestfalen-Lippe, 2011.

[67] Kasper, Birgit: "Demographischer Wandel und Wohnbiographien. Ansprüche an gemeinschaftliche Wohnformen," Special issue, *Wohnbund-Informationen* 2, nos. 4–5 (2007).

[68] Wriedt, Verena: "Möbel und Räume – Design- und Produktionsprinzipien," in Fleischhauer and Wriedt, Wohn-Vision-2020 (see note 66).

[69] Deutsche Gesellschaft zur Holzforschung e. V., ed.: *Informationsdienst Holz: Ökobilanzen Holz. Fakten lesen, verstehen und handeln*, Munich, 1997.

[70] Energie Agentur. NRW (2007): Energieeffizienz in der Holzbe- u. verarbeitenden Industrie. Internet: http://www.ea-nrw.de/unternehmen. Accessed May 4, 2010.

Funding organization:
DBU – Deutsche Bundesstiftung Umwelt gefördert durch www.dbu.de

Project initiator and leader: Dr Werner Baumann, TU Dortmund University, Institute of Environmental Research (INFU)

Project partners:
Hochschule Ostwestfalen-Lippe, Detmold School of Architecture and Interior Design; Academy of Design and Crafts, Münster; ecomoebel GmbH, Dortmund; School of Art and Design Kassel, Industrial Design Werkhof gGmbH, Hagen; RecyclingBörse! Herford

Wohn-Vision-2020 website:
www.hs-owl.de/wohn-vision-2020/

Facade Recycling

[71] Hegger, Manfred; Fuchs, Matthias; Stark, Thomas; Zeumer, Martin: *Energieatlas*. Basel: Birkhäuser, 2007.

[72] German Renewable Energy Sources Act, text in German: http://bundesrecht.juris.de/bundesrecht/eeg/gesamt.pdf

[73] Arztmann, Daniel: *Recycling of Facade Systems*. Detmold: Hochschule Ostwestfalen Lippe, 2010.

[74] VDI2243 | Recycling oriented product development; Verein Deutscher Ingenieure, Düsseldorf; 2002.

Measuring Light – Calculating Geometry

[75] Ibelings, Hans: *Supermodernism. Architecture in the Age of Globalization*. Rotterdam: NAi Publishers, 1998.

[76] Mikell P. Groover: *Fundamentals of Modern Manufacturing: Materials, Processes, and Systems*. Upper Saddle River, NJ: Prentice Hall, 1996.

Notes

Digital Design and Construction

[77] Schmitt, Gerhard: *Architektur mit dem Computer*. Braunschweig: Vieweg, 1996, pp. 28–31.

[78] On this, see also: Hauschild, Moritz; Karzel, Rüdiger: *Digitale Prozesse*. Munich: Detail Verlag, 2010.

[79] Supervised by: Prof. Marco Hemmerling and Prof. Ulrich Nether, 2009.

[80] SunSys was awarded the Studienpreis BDA Masters 2009.

[81] Supervised by: Prof. Marco Hemmerling and Prof. Swantje Kühn, 2008.

[82] www.rhino3d.com, www.grasshopper3d.com.

[83] Schindler, Christoph: "ZipShape – A Computer-Aided Fabrication Method for Bending Panels without Molds," in Architecture "in computro" [26th eCAADe Conference Proceedings], Antwerp 17–20 September 2008.

[84] Supervised by: Prof. Marco Hemmerling, Prof. Holger Hoffmann and Prof. Matthias Michel, 2011.

[85] On this, see also: Pottmann, Helmut; Asperl, Andreas; Hofer, Michael; Kilian, Axel: *Architectural Geometry*. Exton, PA: Bentley Press, 2007.

[86] Buckminster Fuller, Richard: *Operating Manual for Spaceship Earth*. Zurich: Lars Müller, 2008.

[87] Hensel, Michael; Menges, Achim: "Form- und Materialwerdung," ARCH+, no. 188 (2008): p. 18.

[88] Hemmerling and Tiggemann, *Digital Design Manual* (see note 25).

The Printed Building Envelope

[89] ASTM, Typologies for layered fabrication processes, in ASTM F2792, A. USA, Editor. 2009, ASTM International Committee F42 on Additive Manufacturing Technologies: Annual Book of ASTM Standards, Volume 10.04.

[90] Strauß, Holger: *AM Facades – Influence of additive processes on the development of facade constructions*. Detmold: Hochschule OWL - University of Applied Sciences, 2010: p. 83.

[91] Mattheck, Claus: *Verborgene Gestaltgesetze der Natur: Optimalformen ohne Computer*. Karlsruhe: Karlsruhe Institute of Technology, 2006, p. 116.

[92] Hopkinson, Neil; Hague, Richard and Dickens, Philip: *Rapid Manufacturing. An Industrial Revolution for the Digital Age*. Chichester, England: John Wiley and Sons, Ltd., 2006.

[93] Knaack, Ulrich; Bilow, Marcel; Strauß, Holger: *Imagine 04 – Rapids: Layered Fabrication Technologies for Facades and Building Construction*. Rotterdam: 010 Publishers, 2010, p. 128.

[94] Wohlers, Terry T.: "Review of Current US AM Market," TCT Magazine, April 2011.

[95] Honsel, Gregor: "Drucken in 3D," *Technology Review* (2006).

Picture credits:
All illustrations reproduced here are the property of the author.

References:
Footnote to [89]: ASTM International Committee F42 on Additive Manufacturing Technologies: AM: ~ process of joining materials to make objects from 3D model data. Additive Manufacturing (AM) as opposed to subtractive manufacturing methodologies. Usually with AM, parts are processed layer upon layer. Synonyms: additive fabrication, additive processes, additive technologies, additive layer manufacturing, layer manufacturing, and free-form fabrication.]

Footnote to [90]: cf. Holger Strauß, internal concluding report "Influence of Additive Processes on the development of Facade Constructions," Hochschule OWL – Kawneer-Alcoa third-party project; presented in October 2010.

Project partners:
Kawneer-Alcoa Europe Commercial SAS, La Plaine, France; Kawneer-Alcoa Aluminium Deutschland, Inc., Iserlohn, Germany; Alcoa Architectuursystemen, Harderwijk, the Netherlands

The contribution and the project "The Printed Building Envelope" has been supported by:

The contribution and the project "Connections and Coatings" has been supported by:

Gefördert durch:

aufgrund eines Beschlusses des Deutschen Bundestages

The contribution and the project WohnVision-2020" has been supported by:

gefördert durch

Deutsche Bundesstiftung Umwelt

www.dbu.de

Authors

Daniel Arztmann Director of technical development for growth markets at Schüco International KG, Bielefeld since 2011. 2010 team leader and project engineer in Schüco's Engineering Europe department. 2010 Master's in facade engineering, Hochschule Ostwestfalen-Lippe, Detmold. 2003 Diploma in architecture, specializing in metal construction, Hochschule für angewandte Wissenschaft und Kunst Hildesheim-Holzminden-Göttingen (HAWK). Since 2010 master's course lecturer for International Facade Design and Construction (IFDC). Member of the European Facade Network (EFN).

Jan Bieniek At the Detmold Schule für Architektur und Innenarchitektur, Hochschule Ostwestfalen-Lippe since 2006. 2010 Bachelor of architecture and interior design, since his MA interior design and architecture. Student or academic assistant in the model-making and prototype manufacturing department since 2007.

Thomas Böhm Architect, project director, and member of the Böhm Gruppe research department, Potsdam, Germany, since 2009. 2009 architecture diploma at the Hochschule RheinMain University of Applied Sciences Wiesbaden Rüsselsheim Geisenheim, long stays in the USA, Austria, and Spain.

Jens Böke MA Since 2012 coordinator of the postgraduate Master – Computational Design and Construction" and since 2013 project director and research associate in the ConstructionLab at the HS-OWL in Detmold. 2012 Start of studies for a doctorate in the field of CAAD at the TU Delft. 2009 BA at the HS-OWL, Detmold School of Architecture and Interior Architecture. 2012 MA at the msa, münster school of architecture. 2008 traineeship in the dutch architectural design office UNstudio.

Dr. Thomas Braig Since 2009 head of Bayer MaterialScience's EcoCommercial Building Program in Europe, Middle East, and Africa (EMEA). 2005–09 Asia Pacific regional marketing director for Diversified Industries in the Polyurethanes business unit, Bayer AG, Hong Kong. 2002–05 management assistance and personal assistant to various executives. 2000–02 laboratory head for semicrystalline thermoplastics in the research & development department of the plastics group at Bayer AG. 2000 PhD in polymer chemistry from the TU in Munich, Germany.

Xavier Ferrés Padró Diploma in architecture at Escola Superior d'Arquitectura del Vallés (Polytechnic University of Catalonia), master's in construction technology from UPC. Since 2006 assistant academic coordinator and teacher of the Master de Arquitectura de Fachadas at the University of the Basque Country (EHU). Head of Ferrés Arquitectos & Consultores, consulting office in Spain related to facade building and technology for more than twenty-five years.

Dr. Mark Fleischhauer Since 1998 researcher at the TU Dortmund University at the Department of Regional and Urban Economics, Faculty of Spatial Planning (1998–2003), the Institute of Spatial Planning (IRPUD, since 2003) and the Institute of Environmental Research (INFU, 2007–11). 1997 diploma in spatial planning at the University of Dortmund, 2003 doctorate thesis.

Eckard Foltin Director of the new business creative centre at Bayer MaterialScience AG since 2003, since 2008 within global corporate development. Since 1984 various positions from application technology to marketing in the plastics field in various regions for Bayer AG. 1984 Diploma in mechanical engineering / process technology.

Christian Grabitz Director of marketing and communication for the WIB Wirtschaftsvereinigung Industrie- und Bau-Systeme e.V. (Commercial Association for Industrial and Building Systems) since 2009, responsible for publicity for the WIB's specialist building associations – and also for the steel profile grids working party. General secretary of the European Door and Shutter Federation e.V. 2006–2009 assistant director and later head of quality in the motor car supply industry. 1997–2001 studied economics and organization sciences specializing in marketing and logistics at the Universität der Bundeswehr, Munich, and the University of Texas, Austin.

Marco Hemmerling Professor of computer-aided design and director of the postgraduate master's course on computational design and construction at the Detmold Schule für Architektur und Innenarchitektur, Hochschule Ostwestfalen-Lippe. Architecture diploma at the Bauhaus-Universität Weimar and the Politecnico di Milano. Postgraduate MA in architecture media management at the Hochschule Bochum. Member of the Bund Deutscher Architekten and the Deutscher Werkbund.

Thomas Henriksen Thomas Henriksen works for Waagner-Biro as Research & Development Director, responsible for the R&D department. Developing new structural concepts and researching the use of new materials in facades. He has gained a high level of experience in design across a wide range of buildings and infrastructure projects. He has been working as a project manager on several big projects including the facade works for the Harpa concert hall in Reykjavik and recently the Sowwah Gallaria in Abu Dhabi. Thomas Henriksen is currently attached to the TU Delft as a guest researcher.

Dr. Winfried Heusler Since 1998 technical director for Aluminium and CTO (Chief Technical Officer) at Schüco International in Bielefeld, Germany. 2004 Professor at the architectural faculty of the University of Kiev, Ukraine. 2002–04 lecturer at the University of Stuttgart, Germany. 1981–98 facade construction company GARTNER, Germany. 1991 doctorate at the Technical University of Berlin, Germany. 1976–81 diploma in mechanical engineering at the Technical University in Munich, Germany.

Linda Hildebrand Studying for a doctorate on gray energy in the building sector at Delft University of Technology since 2008; academic teaching and research assistant at the Hochschule Ostwestfalen-Lippe (HS OWL), Detmold, Germany. 2008 Architecture diploma, HS OWL, architecture and interior design faculty. Career launch into pilot certification work with the DGNB (Deutsche Gesellschaft für Nachhaltiges Bauen; German Association for Sustainable Building). Active in several research projects and publications.

Authors

Christoph Kirch Academic assistant and project director in the ConstructionLab research department at the Hochschule Ostwestfalen-Lippe (HS OWL), Detmold, Germany, since 2008. 2008 examination for authorization to present building documents for interior designers. 2007 Diploma in interior design, HS OWL, faculty of architecture and interior design. Before studying he trained as a cabinetmaker. He specializes in the field of measurement technology for the perception of architecture (Eye Tracking System) and acoustics.

Dr. Ulrich Knaack Chairman of the architectural engineering and technology department in the architecture faculty, TU Delft, Holland, and professor in the construction design department since 2009. Founder of the facade research group at the TU Delft and at the HS OWL. Director of the international facade design and construction M.Eng. program at the Hochschule Ostwestfalen-Lippe (HS OWL), Detmold, Germany, since 2008. Has worked there since 2004 as professor of design and construction, dean of the department in 2011/12. 1998–2005 worked as architect and general planner in various studios in Düsseldorf, including RKW. 1998 doctorate at the RWTH Aachen on structural glass building.

Dr. Lorenz Kramer Since 2008 innovation manager in the Creative Center within New Business at Bayer MaterialScience AG. Representative of Bayer MaterialScience in the open innovation network future_bizz, where new business ideas and business models are developed together with other companies along the value chain. Doctorate in physical chemistry. Studied chemistry at the University of Cologne.

Christina Kröger Since 2008 companion in the architectural office Stellwerkstatt in Detmold, Germany. 2005–08 architect at Fritzen+Müller-Giebeler, Ahlen. 2005 worked for ASTOC Architects and Planners, Cologne. Participating in architectural competitions as well as planning and building construction. 2000–2005 Studied architecture at the Hochschule OWL, Detmold. Student assistant for the chair of urban and city planning. 2004 Practical semester at Stephen Varady Architecture Sydney, Australia.

Aitor Leceta Murguzur Since 2010 research assistant of José Miguel Martínez Rico at the Architecture School of San Sebastian. Since 2009 designer in Samazuzu Arquitectos office. Since 2008 freelancer on architectural visualization. Since 2007 member of M-etxea research team, being responsible for Kimu workshops about digital fabrication and parametric design. He studied architecture at the University of the Basque Country.

Dr. Steve Lo Senior lecturer in sustainable environmental engineering and director of studies for the postgraduate diploma/MSc in facade engineering at University of Bath, England, since 2009. Worked for the Environmental Section of the R&D department of Wimpey Homes and at the Rutherford-Appleton Laboratory of the UK Science and Engineering Research Council. 1990 Doctorate at Cranfield University. 1985 Gained MSc in energy conservation and the environment at Cranfield University.

José Miguel Martínez Rico Since 2006 PhD researcher at the University of the Basque Country (UPV/EHU). Since 2007 teaching at the UPV/EHU in the master's program in light facade architecture and sustainable construction, soil mechanics, foundations, architecture law and project construction. Since 2007 scientific committee of the master's program in light facades. Since 2007 member of M-etxea research team. 2005–08 researcher of the Modern Movement in the Basque Country for DOCOMOMO Ibérico.

Ulrich Nether Professor of product design and ergonomics in the architecture and interior design department at the Hochschule Ostwestfalen-Lippe (HS OWL), Detmold, Germany, since 2006. Since 2008 founder member and spokesman for the PerceptionLab research department at the college. 1998–2005 First partner, then board chairman for the Hadi Teherani, Hamburg, product design brand. Independent interior architect and designer with Jeanette Faust in Düsseldorf since 1992. 1989 Diploma in interior design at the PBSA, Düsseldorf. Numerous national and international prizes such as the gold BR Deutschland design prize 2004, the Neocon Gold Award, various Red-Dot and IF-Awards for product design and the IF-Communication Award. Member of the Deutscher Werkbund.

Dr. Uta Pottgiesser Since 2012 dean of the faculty of architecture and interior design at the Hochschule Ostwestfalen-Lippe (HS OWL), Detmold, Germany. Since 2008 course director of the M.Eng. program in international facade design and construction at HS OWL. 2006–11 Vice president of research, development, and internationalization. Since 2004 professor of building construction and materials at HS OWL, faculty of architecture and interior design. 2002 Doctorate from the department of civil engineering, TU Dresden. 1991 Diploma in architecture, TU Berlin. Since 2005 organization of the annual conference facade200x at HS OWL. Since 2010 member of the Docomomo International Scientific Committee of Technology (ISCT).

Frank Püchner Freelance worker since 2010 in the digital design department, training for 3D modeling, visual representation and desktop publishing. 2010 Diploma in architecture, Hochschule Ostwestfalen-Lippe, Detmold, Germany. Trained as a carpenter before studying.

Lisa Rammig Since 2012 facade engineer at Inhabit Europe, London. 2010–11 ConstructionLab, Detmold School of Architecture, HS-OWL. 2010 Facade Research Group, TU Delft. 2010 MA in architecture and MEng IFDC at Detmold School of Architecture, HS-OWL. 2008 BA in architecture at Detmold School of Architecture, HS-OWL.

Sergio Saiz Since 2008 manager of thermal energy area of TECNALIA and energy engineer at the University of Basque Country (UPV/EHU). Since 2011 member of the Energy Efficiency Enterprises Association Steering Committee and LEED AP for new buildings and major renovations. Since 2004 master's degree in thermal engineering.

Dr. Christoph Schindler Since 2002 partner at schindlersalmerón furniture architecture, since 2010 lecturer at Zurich University of Applied Sciences (ZHAW). 2009 Doctorate at Ludger Hovestadt's chair of CAAD at ETH Zurich. 2000 Diploma in architecture, TU Kaiserslautern, Germany. He held workshops at the Detmold School of Architecture and Interior Design (2011), Royal Academy of Fine Arts in Copenhagen (2010, 2012),

Fachschule für Holztechnik Hamburg (2009), NTNU Trondheim (2006, 2007) and Hochschule Liechtenstein (2006). He is lecturing and publishing on a regular basis.

Dr. Holger Strauß Researcher and member of the facade research group at the TU Delft, Netherlands. Course manager of the M. Eng. program "International Facade Design and Construction" at Hochschule OWL, Detmold, Germany. Project leader in research and development. Diploma in architecture at HS OWL. Freelance architect. Certified engineer for care and conservation of historical buildings. Degree as master cabinetmaker. Certified log cabin builder.

Jörn Tillmanns Trained as a stonemason/stone sculptor and then worked as an artist-smith. He concluded his subsequent architecture studies with a diploma and has been a member of the Architektenkammer Hessen since 2011. He has worked for Planquadrat Elfers Geskes Krämer Part.G. since 2000, since 2004 as project manager specializing in design and sustainability.

Verena Wriedt Since 1989 chair of furniture and product design at Hochschule Ostwestfalen-Lippe (HS OWL), Detmold, Germany. 2008–2009 Dean, faculty of architecture and interior design at HS OWL. 2004–2006 Vice dean, faculty of architecture and interior design at HS OWL. Since 2001 head of the school's workshop for experimental modeling. 1981–2001 Freelance with workshop for designing and making wood furniture, Hamburg. 1981 Finished her education at John Makepeace School for Craftsmen in Wood, England. Until 1979 was trained as a cabinetmaker, studied fine and applied art, archaeology, and history in Munich, Berlin, and London.

Dr. Jan Wurm Since 2008 leader of the Europe Region Materials Group of ARUP, Berlin. Being an architect with a deep technical understanding of the building process and products, Jan has steered a number of successful product developments and innovations together with industry partners. 2005–08 Arup Materials Consulting and Arup Facade Engineering, London. 2005 Doctorate in structural glass, RWTH Aachen, Germany. 1999–2005 Leader of glass research group, RWTH Aachen. 1999 Diploma in architecture, RWTH Aachen.

Index

3D model 46, 136ff, 144ff, 168

absorption 95ff
acoustic 95ff
additive fabrication 160, 171
Additive Manufacturing (AM) 159ff, 168
analysis 18ff, 45, 71ff, 95, 124ff, 135ff, 142ff
anchorage system 102ff
art 78ff

Blechprofilroste 60
break 83
building automation 69
building envelopes 60ff, 75ff, 165

Cable net 40
CAD-CAM 26
class A fire protection 95
CNC hot wire cutter 56ff
combinations 128
comparative measurements 98
component facade 42ff
composition 82ff, 169ff
computer technology 24, 140
conceptual phase 27
construction 21ff, 25ff, 34ff
construction types 34
curved forms 53ff
curved glass 79ff

designing process 146
design principles 64ff
design tools 73ff, 134
development 10ff, 24ff, 34ff, 64ff, 87ff, 95ff,
   114, 140ff, 159ff, 170
digital design 27ff, 140ff
digital design process 164
digital form development 25
digital planning instruments 46
digital planning method 147
digital process chain 145, 164
digital tools 24ff, 141ff
drafting process 24ff

energy and materials efficiency 71
energy consumption 42, 115, 124ff, 149
energy flow 133
envelope 133
environment 137
environmental impact 112, 125ff
expanded metals 135ff

fabrication 140ff, 159ff, 168ff
facade construction 102, 129, 165
facade design 66, 134
facade elements 94ff, 117ff, 154
facade functions 42
facade node 164
facades 34ff, 60ff, 70ff, 115ff, 124ff, 134ff,
   148ff, 159ff

facade system 153ff, 160ff
fire resistance 79ff

geometrical 53ff, 136ff, 146
geometry 46ff, 53ff, 65, 133ff, 144ff, 159ff
glass 36ff, 74ff, 78ff, 96ff, 168ff
glass mounting 39
gray energy 125

human-centered design 9ff, 74

increased efficiency 126ff
innovation in construction 34, 48
innovation processes 49
insulating 81, 88ff
integrating 98
interaction 26ff, 79, 140, 154
interdisciplinary 12, 63ff, 73, 92, 95ff
invention 34, 48ff

laminated 54ff, 81ff,168
lattice shell 36ff
LED backlighting 64
load-bearing capacity 63, 79
luminous transmittance 135

manufacturer's capabilities 79
manufacturing process 29, 136, 142, 162
market 16ff, 34, 48, 58ff, 60ff, 87ff, 94ff
materials analysis 128
materials databanks 97
media technologies 24
metal 60ff, 99ff, 134ff, 164, 168ff
metal meshes 134ff
models 79, 136

operating energy 125

parameters 27ff, 36, 48, 94ff, 135ff, 142ff, 169ff
Parts Distribution 39
plastic 128ff, 151ff
polyvalent wall 42, 71
post-and-beam connector 162
potential changes 161
practitioner 73
product-centered design 74
product design 58
product development 30, 63ff, 94, 130ff
production 82, 159
production process 26ff, 108, 125, 143
production technique 31, 58, 114
profile 102, 162ff
programmed parametric models 28
prototype 29, 54, 109, 143, 163
public 37, 95

Radio-frequency identification (RFID) 130
radius-to-material thickness ratio 58
rapid prototyping 26, 159, 166
raw materials 97, 124ff, 152

recycling options 129ff
recycling passport 130
recycling potential of an element facade 127
recycling properties 128ff
Renewable energy 74, 115ff, 127, 153
research process 96
resources 74ff, 107, 124ff
road map 34ff
roof 36ff, 78ff, 122, 151ff

samples 66
Simulación lumínica 138
simulation 135ff, 140, 148ff
solar factor 134ff
solar radiation 118, 135ff, 149
solar thermal effect 117ff
sound absorption 94ff
steel 46ff, 63, 79ff, 146
stiffening 79
strength 81, 170ff
structural element 78, 154
structural glass 80ff
structure model 143
surface 18ff, 55ff, 95ff, 143ff
sustainability 31ff, 71, 111, 124
sustainable network 77

technology-related production implementation 64
thermal 74, 117ff, 134ff, 170ff
thermal breakage 82

user acceptance 103
user groups 63

ventilation and exhaust processes 43

wood 54ff, 144

ZipShape 53ff

Acknowledgments

We would like to thank all authors and partners involved for their support of the publication with texts and images. The critical and constructive examination of the drawings was done by Gabriela Lucia Cadena Salgado and Andrea Peitz. Anne Rotter and Danny Smith helped work on the texts.

The publication has been supported by:

Hochschule Ostwestfalen-Lippe
University of Applied Sciences

Product Development and Architecture
Visions, Methods, Innovations

Uta Pottgiesser, Holger Strauß (eds.)

Project management
Annette Gref, Katharina Kulke

Copy editing
Monica Buckland

Translation German – English
Alison Kirkland

Layout, cover design and typography
Miriam Bussmann, Berlin

Unless otherwise indicated, the figures and
images are by the authors.

A CIP catalog record for this book is available from the Library
of Congress, Washington D.C., USA.

This book is also available in a German-language edition
(ISBN 978-3-0346-0840-4).

© 2013 Birkhäuser Verlag GmbH, Basel
P.O. Box 44, 4009 Basel, Switzerland
Part of De Gruyter

Printed on acid-free paper produced from chlorine-free pulp. TCF ∞
Printed in Germany

ISBN 978-3-0346-0841-1

9 8 7 6 5 4 3 2 1

www.birkhauser.com